Little Red

Book

of

Fire House

Pranks

Volume I

- A side of the Fire Service the public never sees.

by JEFF HIBBARD

Warning - It would be impossible to properly retell some of these classic fireman pranks without using some of the garden variety four letter words commonly heard around any fire station. So, ya might want to read it first before passing this book on to some highly impressionable young person. When this book is eventually turned into a movie, it'll probably be rated PG-13

- TABLE OF CONTENTS -

Disclaimer - None of the characters in the stories that follow are identified by name for some obvious reasons. Often the participants are referred to as Fireman Bob. Captain Jones, or the like to better explain some of the often elaborate preparation and execution of the action described.

- FOREWORD -

"This book is dedicated to firefighters all across our country who regularly charge into situations that most folks are busy trying to get away from."

Your author is part of a large fire department family with members who have served in every promotional rank, including a father who retired after 34 years from the Los Angeles City Fire Department as it's Chief Engineer. Not surprisingly I followed in the Family tradition, serving as a fireman on both the Pasadena and L.A. City Fire Departments before retiring in 1987. So, for as early as I can remember, I've always been around firemen. And of all the fire department stories I've heard over the years, the ones that really caught my interest were not the big fires retold or the impressive new equipment on line, but rather, the hilarious stories about the unauthorized activities which took place back at the fire station between alarms.

If you're reading this book as a fireman please bare with me through the next chapter, as it is imperative that I explain to the non-fireman reader the very unique working conditions that regularly cause apparently well adjusted grown men to occasionally act in a deviant manner. This is not a book about exciting fires or heroic action, it is simply a composite picture of the humorous side of the American Firefighter and what's probably been going on down at your local fire station for years. I hope you enjoy it.

-A typical one story LAFD fire station built in the early 60's. Intended to house a single engine company of 5 to 7 men, its apparatus floor and quarters was built just big enough to accommodate two fire companies and their 10 to 14 firefighters if need be. -

- SETTING THE STAGE -

To most folks firemen are those nameless men often seen working unemotionally at the latest emergency in their brightly colored coats on the evening news. Or, maybe as those brave men charging down the street on a big red fire truck, lights flashing and siren wailing. And ,I'm sure most of you have driven by your local fire station, sometimes with their big doors open exposing the highly polished fire apparatus quietly waiting to respond to the next emergency.   Well....there's something else that has been unofficially going on in most every fire station in this country for years, and this is probably the only place you'll ever see it in print. I'm sure after reading this book, you too will be convinced that America's Firemen are indeed the world's greatest pranksters.

Back in the 1800's as communities became towns, and towns became cities, gradually local governments began allocating money to turn volunteer fire brigades into paid fire departments which would provide round-the-clock on call fire protection. As these population centers grew, so did the number of firemen manning an ever increasing number of fire stations.

As time went by the 3 shift (or platoon) 24 hour work cycle became the standard firemen working schedule in most of the bigger fire departments. This means that at every fire station there are 3 separate crews which take turns being on duty for 24 hours at a time (i.e. A-shift, B-shift, C-shift). In a typical 30 day month, each crew would work 10 shifts, which averages out to about 60 hours a week. The pattern of these 24 hour shifts vary with departments, but they generally go something like this: Work a 24 hour shift, off a 24 hour shift, work a shift, off a shift, work a shift, off 4 shifts, and then repeat. Change of shifts at a fire station generally takes place between 7 & 8 in the morning with no off-going fireman leaving the station until he is relieved by a member from the on-coming shift. This system assures that there is always a full crew to man the fire trucks no matter what time an alarm comes in.

Here are definitions of some common fire department terms that will help you non-firemen better understand the stories that follow.

The rank of fire station personnel begins at the bottom with the **Firemen**, who are the worker bees of the station. **Apparatus Operators** are on the next pay scale rung up the ladder. They operate and maintain the piece of fire equipment that they're assigned to. An **Engineer** does basically the same job as an Apparatus Operator. But, he is also schooled in hydraulics and therefore is almost always assigned to a rig that pumps water. A **Captain** is the leader of the crew and is supposedly in charge of everything that goes on at his fire station when he's on duty. Next up the food chain are the various **Chief Officers** (the Brass). The lower levels of these chiefs are quartered at selected fire stations throughout the areas that the fire department covers. Although each of these chiefs are assigned to a particular station, they are responsible for the activities of not only that station, but a number of other fire stations in the vicinity and the specific areas that all of

8

them together cover. During most of the daytime working hours a chief will be out of his *home* station visiting other stations, or off on other department business. The generic term of FIREMEN is often used to describe all the men at a station, or a fire, or whatever.

-This multi company fire station has a large enough apparatus floor to house 3 long rows of fire apparatus behind its big fire doors. Opened in 1949 in North Hollywood, Fire Station 60 initially provided fire protection for a huge part of L.A.'s San Fernando Valley. Over the years, 60's has continued to house a full complement of men and equipment as development rapidly replaced the orange trees. A two piece engine company, a truck company, a battalion chief and driver, and a rescue ambulance crew, for a total of between 12 & 17 men are on duty at all times.-

Fire trucks? Fire engines? Hook'n'ladders?
WHAT'S WHAT?

OK, here's hopefully an understandable explanation. Stationed down at your typical small neighborhood fire station is most likely an **Engine Company**. This type of company will be made up of one or two similar FIRE ENGINES (or Pumpers) and their assigned crew. These are what most folks think of when they think of a fire truck. And here's where it sometimes gets confusing. The next most common piece of fire apparatus in a fire station is the LADDER TRUCK. When manned by its 5 or 6 man crew, it is generally designated as a **Truck Company**. Both the fire engine and the ladder truck can rightly be called fire trucks, but they are completely different vehicles designed to do a completely different job at a fire.

The above fire truck and its crew makes up the typical **Engine Company**. Although it has a couple of ladders on the side, this type of fire apparatus' purpose is to move water from one spot to another. Using its assortment of different size hoses and its pumps to maintain water pressure in the lines, **Engine Companies** are the ones responsible for getting water on the fire.

Above is a modern Ladder Truck. It's basically an extra long tractor-trailer vehicle with a 'Tillerman' seated in the rear to steer the trailer wheels. You can always spot a fireman assigned to a **Truck Company** by the traditional fire ax strapped to his hip. Forcible entry is still one of his primary jobs at an emergency. With its large selection of various length ladders, including a large 100 feet extension ladder mounted on top, **a Truck Company's** job is to work closely with the engine companies to see that they can effectively get their water into the seat of the fire. **Truck Companies** also carry all kinds of rescue equipment such as a cutting torch, jaws of life, rotary saw, porta power, and the like so they can rescue individuals from even the most unimaginable situations. Most fire departments field about twice as many **Engine Companies** than **Truck Companies**. And naturally, *Truckmen* often take a special pride in being the guys in charge of brute force at a fire. The term *Hook'n'ladder* came from the Pompier and roof ladders, both with metal hooks on one end, that most **Truck Companies** carry. The **Chief's Car** is normally a full sized American sedan with all the extra lights, siren, and radios. A lot of fire stations will also have a **'Plug Buggy'** assigned, which is basically a pick up truck with various attachments.

Turnouts - Whether a firemen is in bed, in the shower, or out playin' handball, his turnouts are never far away. They are made up of a pair of steel soled knee high waterproof rubber boots. Down around these boots are folded the pants legs of a sturdy pair of waterproof canvas pants, complete with suspenders. With a T-shirt and a pair of socks laid on top of these, a neat bundle is created that is easy to carry around with the loops built into the tops of the boots. When an alarm comes in, the undressed fireman simply slips on his socks, sticks his feet down into the boots, and pulls up his turnout pants. Then, while heading for the fire truck, he puts on his shirt and pulls on his suspenders. At the truck, his turnout coat and helmet are waiting for him right where he hung them at the start of his shift. This unique tried and true method allows a fireman to get caught in even the most compromising positions and still get aboard the fire truck in a timely fashion ready to go to work.

To further explain these unique working conditions, let's follow a fireman through a typical 24 hour shift: He arrives at work about 7 AM and heads for the kitchen to coffee up and read the morning paper, while waiting to relieve his off-going counterpart. Eventually his just awakened fire bud emerges from the crew's quarters, gives him a quick run down on what's happened during the past 24 hours, and then at some point says "OK man, you got it". One fireman's shift ends, and another one's starts. This is a process that goes on 365 days a year, at thousands of fire houses around the country.

Generally, the morning officially begins with a meeting where the Captain explains the planned schedule for the day, then the crew turns to performing their routine duties. The Captain regularly retires to his front office to do his paperwork and phone calls. The Engineer or Apparatus Operators, start cleaning, checking, and maintaining their apparatus. And the Firemen, numbering anywhere from 2 to 4 start cleaning up the fire station, toilets and all! This represents a typical single engine fire station and it's 4 to 6 man crew. Some bigger fire stations house multi companies, an ambulance, and maybe a chief's car. Plus a total crew of 20 or more. But whatever the size, the basic individual responsibilities essentially remain the same.

After the daily chores are done, the Company(s) as a whole will generally turn to an organized activity like having an outside drill, testing fire equipment, changing wet hose, etc., etc. Around about noontime, the Cook will give out a call for lunch and all activities will temporarily come to pretty much an immediate stop.

Now before I get ahead of myself, let me give you a tour of what you'll find inside a fire station. On the following pages I've included drawings of typical floor plans of both a single engine fire station and a multi company fire station. Obviously not all fire stations are alike, but they all have to accommodate certain basic needs.

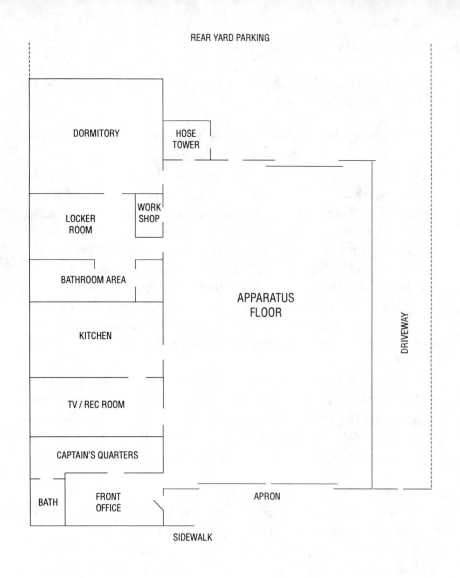

REAR YARD PARKING

DORMITORY

HOSE TOWER

LOCKER ROOM

WORK SHOP

BATHROOM AREA

KITCHEN

APPARATUS FLOOR

DRIVEWAY

TV / REC ROOM

CAPTAIN'S QUARTERS

BATH

FRONT OFFICE

APRON

SIDEWALK

FLOOR PLAN -- TYPICAL ONE-STORY STATION

NOT TO SCALE

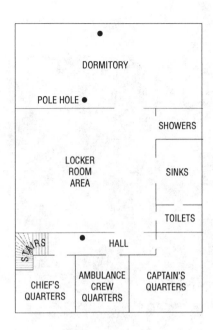

DORMITORY

POLE HOLE ●

SHOWERS

LOCKER
ROOM
AREA

SINKS

TOILETS

STAIRS

● HALL

CHIEF'S
QUARTERS

AMBULANCE
CREW
QUARTERS

CAPTAIN'S
QUARTERS

**TYPICAL
2ND FLOOR LAYOUT**
←

**TYPICAL
FIRST FLOOR LAYOUT
OF 2 STORY
FIRE STATION**
→

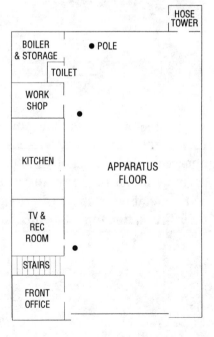

HOSE
TOWER

BOILER
& STORAGE

● POLE

TOILET

WORK
SHOP

KITCHEN

APPARATUS
FLOOR

TV &
REC
ROOM

STAIRS

FRONT
OFFICE

NOT TO SCALE

Although fire stations come in all shapes and sizes, they all have some basic characteristics in common. One of those is an apparatus floor big enough to park all their fire trucks (apparatus) securely in out of the weather. Here an engine company, in front of their station, stops traffic long enough to move the rig back in their fire station, onto the apparatus floor.

Almost all fire stations will consist of the following:

-A FRONT OFFICE to meet the public and conduct station business.

-The CAPTAIN'S QUARTERS, which provides management with it's own bed and bathroom facilities. these are generally, but not always, adjoining the station's front office.

-A TV ROOM not only serves as the crew's lounge, but also provides an area to hold meetings, conduct blackboard drills, etc.

-The KITCHEN acts as more than just a place to cook and feed the crew, it is also the social center of every fire station.

-The CREW'S QUARTERS consists of a locker room, a toilet/shower area, and a dormitory with at least enough beds for one complete crew.

-An APPARATUS FLOOR big enough to park the number of fire vehicles assigned to the station.

-FIRE POLE. A number of multi company fire stations are two stories or more, with the crew quarters upstairs. Hence the pole.

-A typical TV/Recreation room in a multi company fire station-

OK, lets get back to that fireman who we are following through a 24 hour shift. After lunch and a little down time, the whole company will often go back to some organized activity at the fire station or out in their district. And, then again, sometimes they won't. The scheduled work for our firefighter officially ends around 5 PM when the Cook announces that dinner's ready. Now, as you may have noticed, I have not included any fire alarms in this first 9 hours of his shift. But, whenever one does come in, the entire crew drops everything and jumps on the fire trucks and leaves. Including the Cook. No matter if you're just sitting down to eat, in the shower, or sittin' on the toilet....everybody gets up and goes!

After dinner the firemen are generally on their own. Some spend this time studying for promotional exams, watching TV, or whatever. Others may just sit around over a cup of coffee bullshittin' and thinking up new ways of having a little fun at somebody else's expense. As the evening whiles on, each of the crew takes a pre-made bedroll (commonly known as a *fart sack*) out of his bedding locker and rolls it out on one of the beds in the dormitory. An then, one by one, everybody finally goes off to bed.

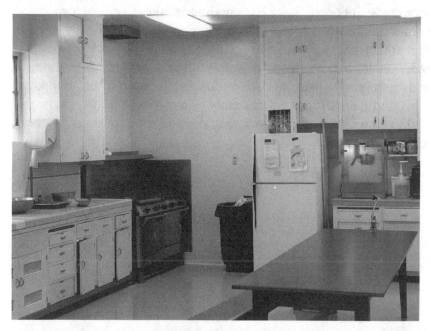

-Photo shows only about half of the large kitchen area in a multi company fire house. Between 15 and 20 hungry firemen will eat a lunch and dinner meal every shift in this setting.-

The next morning, after being lucky enough to sleep through the PM portion of his shift, our fireman arises, rolls up his fart sack and stores it away. He then eventually makes his way to the kitchen to get some coffee and hunt up his relief. After finding his replacement, it's "OK man, you got it", and our boy's off duty until the morning of his next 24 hour shift.

Now I'm not a psychologist, so I can't say for sure why seemingly innocent working conditions like I've just described would produce pranksters galore, but they do. I personally think it has something to do with hiring a bunch of very competent individuals, making them live very close together while training and retraining them to do a dangerous and often unknown job....and then telling 'em basically to hang loose and wait for the bell to ring. Well, hang loose they do, and sometimes in the most mischievous ways.

- THE MONKEY -

Fire Station 93 faces out onto a busy Ventura Boulevard as it stands ready to protect the community of Tarzana in Los Angeles's San Fernando Valley. This large brick one story fire station houses a 2 piece engine company, a hook'n'ladder truck, and a rescue ambulance, with about a 13 man shift assigned to man this equipment. On this particular summer weekday afternoon, the whole crew was much more interested in getting another chance at their latest prank than the routine fire house activity they were working on. After each of their previous attempts, which produced varied results, the crew had hashed over their performances and promised the ring leaders they'd do better the next time.

Next time came unexpectedly when two young ladies wandered in through the big open apparatus doors and asked if they could see a certain single member of the crew. After the girls were assured that the bachelor they were looking for was there, both of them were ushered towards the kitchen as a call went out over the station PA system, "Hey Bill, ya got visitors in the kitchen, soda pop", (*"soda pop", or some other P.A. system code means ladies in quarters).*

In a few short minutes the girls are comfortably seated at the kitchen table and basking in the attention of most of the crew, who have all coincidentally decided that it was now time for a coffee break. As the ladies asked young Fireman Bill the common questions about life at a fire station, the kibitzing crew injected comments into the conversation intended to embarrass their comrade. Laughs all around. Someone brings the girls sodas. The women relax and join in on the fire house banter, confident now that nothing could happen to them in a fire station. Hah!

Gradually, as the various conversations in the kitchen continue, an irregular knocking-like sound from behind an adjoining wall slowly grows loud enough that one girl finally asks, "What's that?"

"It must be the monkey", answers a fireman standing up near the sink.

"You guys got a monkey?", excitedly inquires the other girl.

"Sure we do", agrees the whole crew.

"No way", say the girls.

One of the firemen at the table begins the story. "No, seriously, we brought a monkey back from our last run." The girls quit laughing and start listening intently to a tale that each one of the firemen in the kitchen takes a part in telling. The girls are told a story of the Company's' last alarm to assist a woman who had some stuff cookin' on the stove when she was chased out of the house by a monkey. She met the fire trucks at the curb, explaining that her husband's monkey had gotten loose and she was afraid to go back in the house to turn off the stove. The firemen described in vague yet heroic detail about how they fearlessly entered the house, armed with only a tarp and blankets, and not only subdued the beast, but rolled it up into a tight bundle and took him out onto the front lawn.

After the emergency had been abated the firemen wanted to return the monkey to it's cage, but this woman would have no part of it. "I don't care what you guys do with it, but that monkey ain't coming' back in here"! When the Captain called for an Animal Control Unit, he was told they were all busy and he might not get one for well over an hour. After reassuring himself on the status of their captive, the Captain got back on the radio and told the dispatcher to send the next available Animal Control Unit to Fire Station 93's quarters. After all, it was getting close to lunch and he wanted to get the Cook back to the station The crew then loaded up the monkey and headed back to quarters. At this point the knocking on the wall has gotten a little louder.

"Maybe we oughta feed him", suggests one fireman. The Captain gets up from the table and says he's gonna give Animal Control another call. They explain to the girls that they put the monkey in a closet in the adjoining TV room. At this point the irregular knocking becomes a banging. About this time, the Captain returns from his call and explains to no one in particular that Animal Control is still tied up.

"I think we can spare a head of lettuce", volunteers the Cook.

"Yeah, lets feed it", agrees the crew.

The primeval banging is now starting to rattle the pictures on the kitchen wall.

As the Cook digs a head of lettuce out of the refrigerator and tosses it to one of the *monkey feeders*, everyone in the kitchen gets up and starts moving into the adjoining TV room. The location of the noise is now obvious to the girls, as they see a straight backed wooden chair wedged tightly under the door knob of a small closet. The banging noticeably stops as the group starts to filing into the TV room. As an impromptu feeding team of 3 firemen get organized, the rest of the group forms a loose semi-circle around to watch. The girls are of course ushered right up near the front. And right about here, the girls finally start asking about the actual size of this monkey. On each occasion they receive vague replies like, "well, it's kinda hard to judge, ya know they're always sorta crouched down, and they got all that hair, and...."

The 3 firemen at the closet door finally settle on a plan. One fireman will remove the chair. One will open the door just a few inches, as the third will pitch in the lettuce. And then quickly, the door will be slammed shut and the chair replaced. The girls are urged up closer, "so hopefully you'll be able to catch a glimpse of him".

There was definitely a tenseness in the room as the fireman holding the chair asks, "OK, you guys ready? Lets do it"! In an impressive fluid motion the chair is pulled away, the door is pulled open slightly, the head of lettuce is tossed in, the door is pushed closed. Well, almost. Something is keeping it from closing. The lettuce tosser quickly steps forward to help. Concerned voices rise as the third fireman drops the chair and lends his shoulder to a door that now seems to have no intention of closing. The girls, sensing that all is not going well, start to back away, but are kinda blocked in by the other firemen standing behind them. Time seems to stand still in 93's TV room as 3 grown men struggle against the door to keep whatever is in there from getting out.

Suddenly there's a loud angry noise from inside and the door bursts open, throwing the 3 firemen aside. Then, from out of the dark closet jumps a huge gorilla! As this big silver and black haired monster lands only a couple of feet in front of the women's unbelieving faces, it lets out a growl and reaches out for them......and then all hell breaks loose!

Both girls immediately start screaming as they turn and start clawing their way through the firemen behind them. One girl runs back into the kitchen, where she is corralled by a couple of firemen. The other one ran out of the TV room through a door to the apparatus floor. Typically, not being able to leave well enough alone, the fireman in the gorilla suit chased the still screaming girl out onto the apparatus floor, with the rest of the crew following close behind.

They say it was about here that some of the guys recognized a potential flaw in this most excellent prank. Nobody had closed the station's big front doors! As the hysterical woman took another look back, she saw the gorilla was still right on her ass. Her screams then seemed to go up another octave as she ran right out through the opened front doors and into 4 lanes of moving rush hour traffic.

A whole station full of firemen watched as the possible end of their fire careers played out right before their eyes. The squealing tires and honking hours seemed to last forever. This panicked young lady miraculously made it across the boulevard and ran into the first store she came to. But, even more amazing than that, was

25

that none of the skidding drivers hit each other. As the traffic slowly started moving again, somebody pushed the 'close' button and the big doors slowly started moving together. Mercifully shutting the slack jawed firemen off from the angry motorists outside.

- FOLLOW UP -

A couple of firemen quickly went across the street and calmed down both the fleeing woman and the excited store clerk. And then, back at the Fire Station, the girls were soothed with a ride on the fire truck, an invitation to dinner. Plus, a promise to include them the next time the fire guys scared the hell out of somebody else with the monkey. The last probably being the clincher. Sadly, but under extreme pressure from the captains, the gorilla suit was returned by whoever had the buddy over at Universal Studios and never seen again.

Fire Station 93, where the preceding monkey story took place, was for a long time known as one of L.A. City's real *'fun houses'*. When one of it's long time ringleaders retired, his old crew responded on the first shift he was gone, to a reported trash fire a couple of blocks away. When they got on scene, they found a pile of clothes blazing away in the middle of a residential 4-way stop. After dousing the flames, they discovered that the clothes were firemen's uniforms, name tags and all!

- WATER -

As the tool most often used by firefighters in their job, it is not surprising that water is often used in fire house pranks. But, just getting somebody wet is not the real success. It's douching somebody down without them knowing who did it. Multi story fire stations are notorious for the 'bucketing' of the unaware. This could be as simple as one fireman pouring a bucket of water out of a second story window, or off the roof, onto another fireman below. But it would obviously be a lot more effective if, say your victim is standing out front and the street is full of slow moving traffic. Or, better yet, if he's busy ogling some young lady walking by. But, by far the best, is setting something up so the victim triggers the soakin' himself.

THE LOCKER ROOM SHOWER is an excellent example of the latter. The typical firemen's locker found in a fire station locker room consists of a full length cabinet locker for clothes and personal gear, with a smaller bedding cabinet directly above. This same basic cabinet design is also likely be found in other areas of the fire house.

This prank takes a little time while the intended victim is out of the area, but not a whole lot. After gaining entrance, the upper cabinet is emptied and a small hole is drilled through the partition separating the main locker and the overhead cabinet. Next ya need a piece of string, a small stick, and a plastic wastepaper basket. Feed the string down through the hole and connect it to the inside of the lower door, and then close that door. Fill the wastepaper

27

basket about half full of water, and with your stick, tilt and support it in the upper cabinet (facing outward, of course). After adjusting the length of the stick and the amount of water so you can get it to sit steady, position the container as far forward in the cabinet as you can get and still close the door. Next, take most of the slack out of the string coming up through the hole, and tie it to the bottom end of the stick. And finally, remove the hasp or magnet from the inside of the upper door and close it. If the door doesn't want to stay shut, use a small sliver of cellophane tape.

At this point, the only thing needed is to find yourself an inconspicuous place to watch, and start practicing how not to look suspicious. If everything works right, when the intended victim returns and opens his main locker door, the string connected to it will pull the stick out in the bedding locker above. Then, the weight of the tipping waste basket will push the upper door open and about a gallon of water will come gushing down from above, thoroughly drenching your ol' fire bud.

The variations to this prank are endless. Only limited by lack of time and innovation, things firemen have plenty of. Any partially opened regular sized door can easily be rigged to support a plastic kitchen container full of water that will thoroughly wet the bald spot of the first one through it. The following are four other examples of the innovative uses of water by fire house pranksters:

CAR WASH - Often a fire station will have one member who is a compulsive car washer. So naturally, he will often become a prime target of the second floor water throwers. Occasionally the car washer will not give up his habit easily. I remember one fireman who thought he'd beat the bucketeers by moving his vehicle out to the farthest point in the station's parking lot from the building. Then he mocked his tormentors when the thrown water repeatedly fell short. Even when the bucketeers went up on the roof to get more distance they couldn't reach him. But his apparent victory was short lived. On one afternoon, this now confident car washer, bucket and chamois in hand, proceeded out to the sanctuary of the far corner of the side yard and went to work. Little did he know that his tormentors were busy inside insuring that they'd have the last laugh on this compulsive smart ass. Just as our hero was wiping down the last piece of chrome on his pride and joy, someone stuck a 1 1/2" hose line out a second story window and arced a straight stream across the parking lot that thoroughly soaked down both of them. I can still picture him, chamois still in hand, as he vainly fought off the hose stream while trying to roll up his windows.

THE TRULY BOLD & DEVIOUS - Picture a 2 story fire house with the second floor a little smaller than the first. In other words, when you looked out the 2nd floor side windows on one side, right below stretched out about 15 feet of the first floor's roof. To one particular prankster this unusual feature presented an irresistible opportunity. It was an August summer night in L.A. and the firemen had long since removed all the window screens in their non air conditioned second floor crew's quarters. At some point during the night, when about half the guys had gone to bed and the other half were still downstairs watching TV, our prankster went to work. First he gathered up three plastic wastepaper baskets and a broom stick and stashed them in one of the shower room. Then, he filled all of the baskets about half full of water. This shower room was just a couple of rooms down from the dormitory. He then climbed out the shower room window on to the partial first floor roof, taking all his stuff with him.

Then, with the utmost of patience, he repeatedly tiptoed down the roof and reached through the open dormitory windows to carefully balance a waste basket on the metal headboard of an occupied bed. Finally, when all was set, he went back through the shower room window to his locker. There he undressed, got a towel, and went back into the shower room and turned one of them on. Now in the nude, he once again climbed out the shower room window, grabbed his broom stick, and crept to the other end of the roof. Then, taking off in a trot, he poked the broom stick through each window as he passed, knockin' the waste baskets over and drenching the sleeping firemen. He then threw his stick off the roof and dove through the shower room window, shutting it behind him. As a commotion was erupting in the dormitory, our hero got into his already running shower and soaped up from head to toe.

Back in the dormitory a hell of a commotion had broken out. After somebody finally turned on the lights, four soaked and angry firefighters immediately saw that they'd been had and charged out of the dormitory in search of the culprits. A couple of them went out on to the roof area, while the others ran into the locker room areas. One of the first spots to be searched was the shower room, where they flung open all the shower doors. but, they left quickly after finding only one guy, obviously in the middle of his shower. *This is an excellent example of a perfect prank.*

THE PAY BACK - This incident involved 103's, a single engine house located near the Van Nuys Airport in Los Angeles' San Fernando Valley. Fireman Larry worked the first half of his regular 24 hour shift over at LAFD's Helicopter Unit as a trainee, then came over to 103's in the PM to ride the tailboard and hopefully get some sleep during the rest of his shift. This routine continued on for a long time before a regular helicopter spot opened up. Eventually, their fire bud was promoted to the rank of Pilot and assigned full time over at the Helicopter Unit. The guys at 103's had a promotional dinner for him and wished him well.

A few weeks later the Engine Company was called out to help fight a brush fire in the local foothills. And, as the radio chatter soon told them, their old pal Larry was also working this fire, but now as a pilot of one of the Department's water dropping helicopters. After the fire was surrounded and pretty much under control, 103's found itself under the flight path of the choppers going back and forth from their water source to the remaining hot spots on the next ridge over. It didn't take long for Larry to spot his old crew, and for them to spot him. From then on waves were regularly exchanged during every low level pass. After awhile 103s was told to pick up their hose and make themselves available. Well, just about the time the guys had about gotten everything picked up, their ol' pal Larry made one last pass.

Carrying only a partial load of 30 or 40 gallons, he flew out to 103's rig and made a nice low level circle around while waving at the guys. Then he made his bombing run and doused'em. Although it washed all the dust and mud off, the fire truck and the whole crew had water running out of every orifice. But, worse than that, there was that helpless feeling among the crew of not being able to do a damn thing about it.

About a month later, 103's was out running around in the Valley and decided to stop by the airport and visit Fireman Larry. Something they had done many times in the past. On this particular visit, they found out that Larry and all the rest of the pilots were off on a drill of some kind and the place was fairly deserted. On their way out someone spotted Larry's car in the parking lot and had an excellent idea. Seems long ago Larry had bought an old beater car that he used just to drive back and forth to work and haul stuff. It was an old Ford station wagon with duct tape holdin' the front seat together.

In a flash a plan was concocted. Then, with the speed of an excellently practiced drill, the guys parked their rig right next to Larry's Ford, and dumped about 1500 gallons of water into one of the open windows of his pride and joy. That old rust bucket sat right down on the springs and the tires bulged, as the old gum wrappers and cigarette butts started floatin' up and flowing out over the window sills. Some would say that nothing is sweeter than proper revenge. The fire guys over at 103s would surely agree.

- ANIMALS -

Firemen generally are very kind to animals, but still not above using them in a prank if the opportunity presents itself. Many an off duty firemen have made the mistake of leaving their pet at their fire station for a few hours while off running errands, only to find their pride and joy shaved or dyed in an unusual manner when he returned. Here are some other ingenious examples of firemen playing with animals:

The Lion- There is a 2-story fire station in the City of Pasadena that has a kitchen with an unusual layout. First off, it was on the second floor. Secondly, it only had one way in and out, which was located at one end of the long cooking and eating area.

It was a sunny afternoon and the crew had just finished lunch. While about 5 or 6 guys lingered around the kitchen table bullshittin' and drinking coffee, a number of their fire buds had gone down to the sidewalk in front of the fire station to enjoy a little sunshine. About then a guy walked past the station with a lion on a big chain leash. This naturally caught the firemen's attention, and they soon discovered that this was a friendly old circus lion, toothless and de-clawed, and now the old man's pet. Then, a guy who had just came down from the kitchen, had a great idea. It took only a few minutes of convincing before the whole group was quietly sneaking up the stairs towards the kitchen. When they got close to the kitchen door, the old man took the collar off his pet and motioned the lion into the kitchen.

33

The entrance into the kitchen was on the end of the room with the stove, sinks, countertops, etc. Down at the dead-end end of the room were the large dining tables where a small group of firemen were still kickin' back. As they say, one had to be there to really appreciate the commotion that followed. One can only imagine the changes in attitude that took place in that kitchen when a full grown male lion suddenly sauntered in and stared at the startled firemen. Especially since this beast was squarely between them and the only exit. This immediately produced a great uproar. The screaming and yelling, the sounds of things breaking and furniture being rapidly rearranged gave clear evidence that everybody in there was scared shitless. This included the lion, who promptly ran back out of the kitchen to his owner. As the uncontrollable laughter outside the kitchen reached those inside, the guys inside realized that they'd been had.

Snakes- Most of the crew of this multi company fire station were out in their parking lot this morning while they drilled on some piece of equipment. About the time they were wrapping it up, a street showman wandered in through the open gates with a burlap sack full of snakes. It wasn't long before the snakes were dumped out on the concrete and the firemen were tossin' coins in his cup as the Snakeman went through his routine. As the crowd of firemen grew, it was noticed that fireman Bob was hanging back noticeably. When some of his buds tried to get him up closer, he adamantly refused and moved even further away. It immediately became obvious to all that Fireman Bob was deathly afraid of snakes.

34

During the rest of the shift his fellow firemen tormented their friend by finding an ever endless number of ways of bringing snakes into the discussion of almost any subject. But, not willing to let well enough alone, a sinister plot was hatched. It just so happened that Firemen Bob was generally one of the last guys to go to bed on their shift. With that in mind, after he'd made up his bed and gone back downstairs to watch TV, a 3 foot section cut out of an old garden hose was strategically placed between his sheets.

That night everybody made a point of going to bed before ol' Bob, and were wide awake when he came into the dormitory and made his way through the darkness to his rack. It seemed like forever before he eventually got his turnout boots set and crawled into bed. But nothing happened. Finally he rolled over far enough to make good contact with that smooth cold piece of hose, and flew straight up and out of bed with a blood curdling scream. As soon as he hit the floor, and shed the covers that came with him, he ran out of the dormitory into the locker room. The muffled laughter came to an instant stop when he came back in a moment later with a flashlight in hand. As he carefully worked his way back over to his bed, searching the floor as he went, everybody still religiously pretended like they were still asleep.

Eventually Fireman Bob found the hose and became obviously enraged. Then, with that piece of hose in his cocked right hand, he slowly went from bed to bed shinning his flashlight in each firemen's face. Nary an eyelid quivered, each one knowing full well what might be the result. Finally, irate Bob, muttering that he'd find out who was responsible and fix his ass, gave up on sleeping that night and went back down to the TV room. But I'm sure, even from down there, he couldn't escape the sound of the uproarious laughter that finally erupted in the dormitory after he left.

Frogs- A lot of firemen are hunters and fishermen, and are often bringing in some of what they've bagged for their fellow firemen to sample at work. At this particular multi company fire station, a couple of the guys went 'froggin' and did really well. The next shift they brought a whole big bucket of them in, and really made a mess of the kitchen while cutting them up in the sink. But, all was forgiven when the crew sat down that night to a fine meal of southern style frog legs. During the clean up after dinner somebody had an interesting idea of what to do with all those great frog guts that were headed for the trash.

Shortly after the next shift came on duty they had an alarm come in. The on coming fire guys ran for the trucks, put on their turnout coats and fire helmets, and got aboard. All pretty much routine. Then, as the rigs started to roll, the firemen started reaching into their coat pockets for their gloves and things......only to find them full of frog guts. This resulted in a humorous picture. Imagine a whole parade of big red fire trucks going by red light and siren, with all the firemen aboard jettisoning handfuls of frog parts as they passed.

Monkey on a Leash- Sometimes things don't always go as expected. The big set of double doors were open to the street, and a number of the crew were busy working on the rigs at this multi company fire station. Unexpectedly a man with a monkey walked onto the apparatus floor, asking if he could possibly use the phone. This monkey was about three foot tall and wearing a sturdy harness. Connected to it was a leather leash about 6 feet long with a loop at the other end.

Although not normally for public use, the guys were intrigued with his pet and pointed him towards a small closet that contained the crew's phone. The man looped his end of the leash around the outside doorknob and went inside and closed the door. Now needless to say, anytime you unexpectedly have a fairly good sized monkey tied to a doorknob in a fire station, you're quickly gonna draw a crowd of curious firemen.

The monkey seemed friendly enough, at first. It walked out to the reach of his leash and acted like it wanted to shake hands with the wary firemen. All of whom stood back just far enough so it couldn't touch'em. When the *brave* firefighters finally reached out just far enough to touch his outstretched fingertips, the animal reacted like he'd played this game before. Then, to the delight of the original group of firemen, the monkey started approaching any fireman new to the group with one hand behind his back holding a small loop in his leash. And then, when the newcomer reached out just short of the monkey's out stretched hand, this monkey would let go of the slack he held behind his back and jump forward and grab the startled firemen's hand. Everybody would then laugh like hell as he jerked his hand free and jumped back in shock. After the monkey played this trick on about 3 other firemen, he suddenly seemed to get bored and went back to the end of his leash and unhooked it from the doorknob! The silence was deafening as about 12 firemen looked on slack jawed, then the monkey spun around and charged squealing into the group.

What followed was an embarrassing rout of two companies of L.A.'s finest. Some of them ran out the front doors, some dived into cabs of the fire trucks, and others scrambled up on top of the hose beds. About that time the guy finished his phone call and came back out onto the apparatus floor and called for his monkey. As the monkey quickly returned to his Master's side, they both waved thanks to the still shaken firemen, and went on out the door and disappeared up the street.

FIRE DUCK- Located near the busy intersection of Ventura Blvd. and Laurel Canyon in a plush part of Los Angeles is one of L.A.'s more popular restaurants. Nestled around that busy intersection was also F.S. 78, a single engine fire station whose rear parking lot butted up against one of the Sportsmen Lodge's buildings. The Lodge covered a large area consisting of a number of semi-connected buildings in a garden like setting complete with fish ponds and semi-tame waterfowl.

The 15 firemen who made up the three 5 man shifts were all very familiar with their big neighbor, and early on somebody discovered that if ya got up on the roof right behind the fire station ya could look right down into one of the Sportsman's Lodge's fish ponds. Well.....it wasn't too long before the ladder off the fire truck was often seen late at night extended from the fire station's parking lot up to the roof of the Lodge. And, a couple of firemen, fishing poles in hand, catching carp and monster gold fish outta the fishin' hole below. Naturally they threw back everything they caught, but not before puttin' a notch in one of their fins to identify the dumb ones.

One winter evening about dinner time a white duck wandered into the rear parking lot and was spotted looking through the screen door at the firemen in the kitchen. When one of the firemen offered him some of the crew's salad and some garlic bread crumbs, he came right in like he owned the joint and stayed for dinner. From then on, every night like clock work, that duck seemed to show up for dinner. The crews soon found out that he was staying over at the Lodge during the day, but at dinner time he'd walk out the rear entrance, past the parking valet, through the parking lot and out to the sidewalk on busy Laurel Canyon Blvd. Then it was just a short waddle up to the fire house driveway and around back to the kitchen.

The fire guys started having family members drop by around dinner time to 'meet their duck'. Naturally, somebody finally spray painted some black spots on their mascot and he instantly became known around the Battalion as 78's fire duck. Well, 'Spot' stuck around 78's for quite awhile before he just disappeared. Did one of the many dangers of the city finally get him? Or, as the duck trainers at 78's like to think, he just took off and flew north with all those other stupid ducks.

THE TASMANIAN DEVIL, mongoose, viscous weasel, or a cross between a gila monster and a skunk, are some of the many animals used in this prank. But to pull it off correctly on somebody whose never heard of it, in the supposed security of a big city fire station, and surrounded by people he thinks he can trust, is a perfect example of what a good prank is all about.

A guy drops by the fire station (often a fire buff or retired guy) and is invited into the kitchen for coffee and idle chatter. He'll make his intentions known to some of the older members and together they'll pick a victim (generally a rookie). In awhile all of the other fire guys will be clued in and the rookie will be enticed into the kitchen. About then, the visitor mentions that he caught a strange animal awhile back and maybe somebody here knows what the hell it is. Says he's got it out in his truck. Next thing ya know, there's a wooden and wire enclosure sittin' on the kitchen table. It was about the size of a large shoe box, wooden on one end with a hole entering out into a wire caged area. On the bottom of the wire cage part is some shredded newspaper, a couple of turds and some gnawed up old bones. The creature was obviously hiding inside the box.

"I'm sure he'd go right after ya if he got out", explains the owner as he begins his spiel. A piece of meat is gotten out of the refrigerator and poked through the wire holes in the cage. No response. The owner then shakes and lightly taps on the box and everyone claims to clearly see what looks like the angry twitchin' of a hairy tail just inside the hole. As this show is goin' on, the victim is maneuvered up front and the box is lined up accordingly, i.e. aimed. Finally, the owner of this vicious beast shakes the box one more time.....and trips the release!

In a flash, a spring inside pops the hinged top of the box open and throws a hairy velcroed thing out, complete with bushy tail, which hits the victim in the upper chest and sticks! The laughter in this prank is only limited by the hysterics of the guy frantically trying to fight off his imaginary attacker.

- POPSICLE STICK -

Working 24 hour shifts at a fire station provides some very unique working conditions. Indeed, probably serving in the military would be the closest comparison. Living, working, eating, sleeping, riskin' your neck, and relaxing in close quarters with anywhere from 3 to twenty-some other guys over long periods of time creates some very unusual situations. With a combination of government mandated hiring of females and minorities, and our increasing lawsuit happy society, a lot of things have changed (discussed in next Chapter). But, in the 'old days' the guys sometimes handled personal problems in their own appropriate and sometimes spur of the moment fashion. Here is one good example.

With about 3 or 4 years on the job and working at a multi company fire house in downtown L.A., Fireman Billy was havin' a weight problem and had counted out of the regular company mess on orders from above. He now had to bring his own diet stuff to the station, and was definitely not the happier for it. Meanwhile, back in the regular fire house mess (lunch & dinner meals), the guys started a regular routine of having the cook buy a big box of popsicles for dessert every shift. One night the ever hungry Fireman Billy quietly helped himself to one of the many multi colored frozen treats.

Over a number of shifts, this non-contributing member began to openly help himself to one of the organized mess's many popsicles. As this became a regular nightly habit, the derogatory comments were more numerous i.e.:

"Hey Fatso, you didn't kick in for those". And,

"Hey guys, Blimpo Billy's back into our popsicles".

But, these insults had little affect. Then one night, with most of the guys hangin' out around the kitchen table, somebody noticed that *'the Dieter'* was once again munchin' on one of their popsicles, and one of them made an unkind remark. Fireman Billy then made the biggest mistake of his fire service career.

At this point let me remind ya that there are a number of things that you try never to do at a fire station. One of these is to do something to earn a really stupid nickname. Another one is to foolishly issue a challenge that pits you against the rest of the crew.

As the chatter went back and forth over Billy's unauthorized consumption of the popsicles, one fed up member suggested that, "we oughta take that popsicle stick and stick it right up his ass".

Then, in a moment of complete stupidity, Billy shot back, "Fat chance of that, there ain't nearly enough of ya!" Almost immediately, and with virtually no organization to speak of, all of the firemen in the room jumped on this guy at once. And in just a second he was physically bent over the table, his pants pulled down, butt cheeks spread, and with the ice falling off in the process, a popsicle stick was inserted in his butthole. About that time, after hearing all the yellin', a Captain walked in from the adjoining TV room just in time to see a stunned Fireman Billy pulling up his pants, with colorful chunks of popsicle ice falling out of his cuffs. With no one apparently injured the Captain wisely did a turn around and went on back to his TV, hence avoiding God only knows what kind of paperwork.

Now if getting pounced on by 10 guys who stick a popsicle up your rectum isn't bad enough, hearing the story endlessly repeated around the station is worse. But, far worse than either of these, was the new nickname that followed him from assignment to assignment for the rest of his career. For years after that incident, it was not unusual whenever Fireman Billy got a call at any fire station he was working, for the station PA system to sing out *"Call on the grapevine for Popsicle Stick"*. And then for somebody to ask, "Why do they call him that?" And the story would be repeated again.

- END OF AN ERA -

As you've read this far, and continue on, you'll surely catch yourself asking the question *"How'd those guys get away with stuff like that?"* Well, today you pretty much can't! Virtually all of these stories are out of the 70's and earlier. Then the Federal Government got involved. Affirmative Action injected less quality individuals into the mix. The advent of women firefighters effectively ended the long standing men's club attitude at a lot of fire stations. Those changes, along with the fact that we've all become a much more litigious society has dramatically slowed America's pranksters down. Although not gone, they are a lot more low key today, especially on big city departments.

Today, it's almost laughable what kind of a nightmare the press and a bunch of lawyers could make out of the previously described popsicle stick incident. And worse yet, imagine what your local evening news would sound like if Fireman Billy was a minority, or worse yet, a female. On the other hand, thirty years ago, if two firemen had a bad enough beef to settle, they went out in the handball court alone and settled it. Or, the Captain stepped in and resolved things. Rarely did anyone see any reason to get the *Brass* involved in such fire house matters.

I once worked at a fire station where the guys 'pantsed' a Meter Maid and painted a message on her bare butt, (retold in next section) and nobody got sued, socked, or divorced. There was, of course, quite a bit of commotion, but it was contained to the fire station. I've hid out and listened as a large angry fireman violently bashed his way out of a locked closet, and then helped the rest of the crew rebuild the jam, re-hang the door, and then plaster and paint the damage back to normal. The same went for the equipment. It was not unusual for a whole crew to turn into a body and fender gang if the Engineer backed his rig into a pole and bent a fender. In those days America's fire departments were truly thrilling men's clubs and a lot of us would have gladly worked for nothin' if we could be members. It's of this era from which I write.

- THREE MAN LIFT -

Ideally, the 3 man lift is organized and put into action whenever one of your crew is foolish enough to broadcast his up coming wedding to all his fire buds at work. This is generally some relatively new guy. After a proper amount of rehearsing, it is executed sometime during the last shift before the groom leaves for his honeymoon. The procedure goes something like this:

Sometime during the shift, the soon-to-be-married is joined in the kitchen by some other members of the crew. Over coffee, a typical fire house bullshit session breaks out and the conversation is steered to how much different members can lift. Finally, after going back and forth, one guy tops everybody by flatly stating "I can lift 3 of you guys all at once!" While the intended victim looks on, bets are made and the conversation turns to, *How?*

The *lifter* sits down on the bench with his back to the table and starts directing three of the guys where to position themselves. Of course one of these 3 *weights* is the intended victim, and he is told to sit up on the table behind the *lifter* and put his legs over the *lifter's* shoulders. The other two guys get up on the table on both sides of the victim and grab a hold of his arms as they pretend to get ready to sit on the *lifters* out stretched arms. At a prearranged signal the *lifter* drops his arms and holds the victim's legs tight against his chest. At the same time, the two outside men each tightly secure one of the victim's arms and gently roll back on the table.

What this produces is one very helpless individual laying on his back, with all of his arms and legs solidly held by 3 of his fellow firemen. Then, as planned, the rest of the station's crew pour through the door to assist. Magically, some Indian ink, a small brush, shaving cream, and a razor appear. An old timer once told me that, "When ya use a straight razor, they'll quit wigglin' around the moment ya lay it on their belly".

At this point the groom-to-be's pants are undone and pulled down far enough to expose his genitals. What happens next varies, but generally all his pubic hair is removed and a happy face or some appropriate message is painted on his penis. Indian ink is used because it's almost impossible to get off (it finally wears off), and the use of various colors have allowed would-be fire house artists to do interpretations of red and white barber poles, and the like. While the 'painting' is going on, the guys not directly involved are busy discussing what his bride's gonna say "since he obviously assured her he has a good job".

By the time the ink has dried and he is let go, the victim has long since accepted his plight and retaliation against his buds is put off to some later date. And, the best part of most episodes is that when the honeymooner finally returns to work, everybody gets to hear about what happened when his new bride first spots their artwork. The best one I ever heard was that of a young fireman who got 'painted' just before leaving on a month long cruise. The story of his wife's reaction was funny, but nothing compared to what happened later. Seems he got sick, food poisoning or something, and was rushed to the ship's hospital with painful stomach cramps. During the examination the doctor pulled down his shorts and was confronted with a orange and black stripped penis hanging below a message on his belly that read "suck here". Naturally, something like that ain't gonna be kept a secret for long on a ship. And when the cruise ended, most of those on board had gotten to know our hero as "Tiger".

I worked for a while at a busy Battalion Headquarters in the North Hollywood area of Los Angeles City. This station had an unusually large number of 'hang arounds'. These folks are repeat fire house visitors who stop by for a free cup of coffee and good conversation, commonly cops, City maintenance guys, fire buffs, etc.

One of these was a local meter maid who stopped by often to have a cup and just hang out with the fire guys. She got a big kick out of the fire house pranks that the firemen pulled on each other, so much so that she helped out on a couple of them. Then one day, she stopped by and announced that she was getting married to a cop that weekend. *'Well, what the hell, he'll understand'.* The next thing this lady knew she was face down on the kitchen table in a reverse 3 man lift, and getting "best regards from F.S. 60" painted on the cheeks of her ass. Thankfully the guys were right, and the cop did reluctantly understand. Not surprisingly, though, she quit the habit of stopping by the ol' fire house shortly after that.

- LOOSE CHANGE -

One of the things firemen like to do during the slack time of their 24 hour shift is to watch the activity of the public taking place in front of their fire stations. Down in the skid row areas the fire guys get a kick out of watchin' the winos. In Hollywood they follow the activities of the weirdoes, in other areas they watch the hookers, etc., etc.

As an example, I once worked at a single engine house in the middle of a block that was across the street from a junior college. Naturally, girl watching was one of the crews favorite past times. For a number of years we tried unsuccessfully to get the street maintenance guys to paint a crosswalk across the street right in front of the station, so more of the female students would walk on our side of the boulevard. This effort went so far that at one point we planned on buying some white paint and doing it ourselves late some night. Unfortunately, one of the captains got wind of our plan and put a stop to that idea.

Fire Station 98 was located on a busy street in one of the poorer minority areas of the City. This double house was staffed by predominately white firemen, and the guys enjoyed watching the comings and goings of their black neighbors. One shift an engineer brought in some new super trick epoxy glue from home to repair something on his rig. "This stuff makes a permanent unbreakable bond" he boasted. This, of course, gave another fireman a completely different idea for its use.

It wasn't long before a spot on the front sidewalk was cleaned off right outside the front office's heavily tinted windows. Next, a quarter was glued to the concrete and the tire of the Plug Buggy was parked on it while the epoxy set up. About an hour later, everybody got a fresh cup and crowded in the front office to watch the show. It wasn't long after the truck was removed, exposing the shiny quarter, that the guys got their first customer. A middle aged black gentlemen first tried to bend down and scoop up the coin in stride, but came up empty handed. Then he stopped and made a more concerted effort. First he kicked at it, then pulled out a pocket knife and vainly tried to pop it loose before finally leaving in frustration.

For the rest of the day the front office was full of firemen staring out through the tinted windows, while trying their best not to alert 'the performers' with their laughter. After dinner, the guys returned to their vantage point and found that the coin was still firmly in place. But only for a while. As they watched, a young man who had tried to pick up the quarter earlier, returned with a friend. They also brought a hammer and a screw driver and went right to work. After a couple of minutes of pounding they broke it loose and left.

Now most folks would lose interest at this point and go on about their business, but not a bunch of firemen. That night new plans were made. Next shift, one of the guys showed up sportin' a quarter with a 'spike' silver soldered onto one side. Then, after the morning business was taken care of, the guys were out on the front sidewalk drillin' a hole in the concrete. After the new quarter with its spike was solidly glued in place, the pick up truck was again removed and act two began.

This time the fire guys didn't have to wait too long for a serious challenge. A group of about 4 teenagers came by and all took turns at the 25 cent piece before leaving empty handed. But in no time at all, they returned with some tools. It took'em about 10 minutes, all taking turns at it, before they finally beat the now mangled coin free. Admiringly, the firemen finally had to admit defeat.

- OUR BROTHER POLICEMEN -

Both Firemen & Policemen are *sworn personal* of the government entities which employ them. This provides them with the privileges of that position, but it also exposes them to a unique form of double jeopardy. If, say a City plumber or a County secretary gets into trouble with the authorities, but is found not guilty or the charges dropped, the employees status back at work pretty much returns to normal. But, that's not necessarily so if you're a fireman or policeman. It's not unusual for a member of either one of these groups to be fired through their department's Board of Rights hearing process after being cleared by the regular judicial process.

Every organization of sworn personal in our country has a *conduct unbecoming* rule that is applied in such cases. Here's an example of when a fire or policeman would have to defend himself against their department's Conduct Unbecoming rule: An off duty fireman is riding in a car full of acquaintances when it is pulled over for speeding. During the stop a good amount of illegal drugs is found, and everybody in the vehicle is arrested. During the subsequent investigation, the District Attorney decides that there is not enough evidence to prosecute the off duty fireman, and all charges against him are eventually dropped. But at work, a Board of Rights Hearing would be convened and he would most likely be charged with *conduct unbecoming* a Fireman. In other words, by association with such unsavory individuals, he was obviously guilty of conduct unbecoming a fireman. Despite probably arguing that he didn't know anything about his companions illegal activities. There would be a good chance that the fireman in this example would be fired none the less.

This unusual double jeopardy situation that always hangs over their heads helps to create a unique bond between firemen and policemen that exists all across our country. Firemen and policemen who have never met each other routinely work together with courtesy and respect at both routine and emergency situations. This special relationship manifests itself in many ways. A couple of examples, would be cops generally letting firemen go without a ticket after a traffic stop. And, policemen are regular visitors at fire stations and are pretty much treated just like one of the guys.....and that brings us back to the topic of this book.

At a fire station a cop can kick back for a bit and get a break from *the public*. But, occasionally firemen can be an even bigger pain in the ass. Besides spending a lot of time drinking coffee and bullshitin' with the fire guys in the kitchen, sometimes an officer slips into the TV room to watch a football game or simply take a nap in the back row. Most fire station TV rooms are partially filled with rows of used airplane seats. Motorcycle cops are the most vulnerable after they've settled back into these comfortable seats, because they carry a lot more equipment with them. To get really comfortable, most will stick things like their helmet, baton, radio, etc., under their seat. Patrolman generally leave those things in their hopefully unlocked police car out in the parking lot. But, wherever, opportunities like these play right into a firemen's natural inclination to screw around with the cops.

Many a motor officer has left his favorite fire station oblivious to the fact that the headband of his helmet had been 'dusted' with black graphite. Naturally, the next time he makes a stop and takes off his helmet while writing the ticket, he'll end up asking the irritated motorist for his signature with a goofy lookin' black smear all across his forehead.

Batons are also popular targets of the fire house pranksters. I mean, it's pretty easy to snatch a billy club from a cop snorin' away in an easy chair. And, it's just as easy to put it back unnoticed. While it was away the fire house artist, with masking tape and quick-dry spray paint, can produce some interesting work. The standard LAPD issue black baton often became more than just, say, silver or gold. Straight multi colored strips were a possibility, or maybe an interesting barber pole selection. Sometimes spray glue and a piece of ugly wallpaper would produce a unique floral effect. I know this may sound very juvenile to some, but to watch a still sleepy cop storm off with a pink nightstick is not only hilarious, but it is also kinda reassuring. I mean, both sides have chosen a career that puts their lives on the line at a moments notice, and it's nice to occasionally remind yourselves that life's not all that serious.

At one station the fire guys hauled an officer's motorcycle up to the top of the station's hose tower. They used two ropes attached to the back of a truck to do the job, and left the guy napping peacefully in the TV room while they all went out to do some hydrant testing. When the cop woke up he found his Harley 40 feet up in the air, and obviously not about to untie the ropes and try to lower it down himself. As I can remember, this prank kinda backfired. Being and old timer, this officer simply made a few calls to cover his ass and then headed back into the kitchen to see what his fire buds had in the refrigerator. When the crew came back a couple of hours later, they found their victim in the TV room watchin' golf and busy finishin' off his second piece of pie.

Sometimes firemen are a little more subtle. A loud, but relatively harmless explosion can be easily created with the gas from a truck company's cutting torch. With the flame out, the cutting torch's flammable gas and oxy mixture is used to fill up any small flimsy plastic container. The perfect size to wake up a sleeping policeman is one of those small resealable sandwich bags blown up to about the size of a softball. This inflated bag is then placed under a constable's chair, on top of a piece of paper towel, and then one corner of the paper is lit. At this point it is advisable that all fire personal get out of the room, since occasionally cops will draw their guns when a bomb goes off right under their ass! A strange thing normally happens after all the yellin' stops, the victim usually wants to bring his partner by so the fire guys can pull the same prank on him.

Policemen are not always on the receiving end of fire house pranks. One time a truck company Captain decided to pull the chain of a cocky rookie assigned to the engine company in their multi company fire station. This fire station had limited space in its walled in parking area, so the on-going shifters had to park their vehicles out on the local side streets until the crew they were relieving went home. Then, one at a time, the on-coming shifters would got out and get their cars and move them into the station's yard. During one of these shift change periods an alarm came in for the engine company only, and of course, the on-coming rookie was the first aboard. While they were gone the truck Captain walked out of the station, down to the corner, and up the street until he found the rookie's car. Knowing the kid left his keys in his car for that short period, he got in, found the keys, and moved it about two blocks over, putting the keys back under the seat.

When the engine guys returned, the truck Captain had already clued all of his truck crew in on what was going on. "Let's see if the kid still has that goofy smile on his face when he thinks his car's been stolen". They agreed that the guys on his engine company couldn't be trusted and promised to keep the secret to themselves.

Well, about an hour later, the rookie took off to go move his car into the station. He then came back muttering, "I can't believe it, somebody stole my car". Just as his truck company fire buds were about to start playing him like a song, another "Engine Only" call came over the alarm/PA system and away he went.....still car less! As the engine company roared off red light and siren, the truck guys laughed their ass off and couldn't wait till their victim returned.

One thing about fire house pranks is that they're easy to get started, but often hard to keep control of once they get rollin'. On the way back from their run, the engine company just by chance took a different route home and drove right past the rookie's car. "Hey! Stop! There's my car!" Everybody aboard knew it was a

61

joke when the rookie found his car undamaged and his keys hidden right where he'd left them. But, instead of the quick ending to a good prank, it was now only the beginning of an even better one.

While the engine guys laughed at the rookie, one of them admitted that he'd heard about it earlier and identified the truck Captain as the perpetrator. As the talk among the crew turned to how their rookie could turn this prank around, a patrol car drove up and stopped. An old sergeant in the right seat snapped jokingly at the Engineer "Hey, you guys can't double park here!" Then, in another turn of fate, the engine Captain recognized the other cop as a frequent visitor at his previous assignment. In no time the firemen filled the cops in about the opportunity that was currently presenting itself.

As soon as the engine company got back to the station, the rookie and his captain went straight into the front office. Then, before the truck Captain realized what was goin' on, the rookie had a police dispatcher on the station's business phone. "Yes, I'm a Los Angeles City Fireman. Yeah, they stole it from right outside Fire Station 15." And so on. The truck Captain was stunned. After the rookie hung up his phony call the truck Captain vainly tried to regain control. "Listen, let's not blow this thing up into a bunch of unnecessary paperwork unless it's really stolen." "Whata ya mean Cap", stammered the rookie, "it's gone!" "Well, lets not jump to conclusions", counseled the truck Captain, "maybe you just forgot where ya parked it?" While the truck Captain continued to try to find a graceful way out of this, a black and white pulls up in the front of the station and a big ol' sergeant crawls out with a clipboard.

Before the truck Captain could fess up in the privacy of his own office, the rookie is out of the office and opening up the apparatus doors. "I got a call about a fireman gettin' his car stolen", barked the Sergeant. The rookie greeted him and raved about the Police Department's promptness, then invited the Sergeant back into the kitchen for some coffee while he filled him in on the details. The truck Captain had been had.

As word spread, every fireman in the station decided it was time for a coffee break and headed for the kitchen. At this point, half of the firemen in the kitchen knew of their truck Captain's prank, while the other half were privy to the whole deal. But, everybody was wondering just how much farther the truck Captain would crawl out on the limb he was on. Finally the Sergeant told them that, as a favor to the fire guys, he was gonna bend department rules a bit and issue a priority *All Points Bulletin* to his field units in hopes of finding the rookie's car. At that point the truck Captain threw up his hands and confessed. Then, the Sergeant got out his hand cuffs and started talking about Grand Theft Auto charges. Finally, the engine Captain had mercy on his counterpart and called an end to it, amidst the laughter from the whole room.

Sometimes things do get out of control. At one particular engine house, two of L.A.'s finest often stopped by in their patrol car just to bullshit on the station's front apron. They were a mischievous pair who enjoyed the firemen's humor, and often shared the humor of police work when they had some good stories. One night they stopped by to gab with the fire guys as usual and somebody dumped a bucket of water on them from above. They left in a huff, vowing to get even. During the evening on the next shift, these two cops stuck the nozzle of a dry chemical fire extinguisher through a crack between the apparatus doors and covered the crew's fire engine with an ugly coating of white powder.

That evening, the whole crew turned out to clean up their rig. The truck was pulled out onto the station's front apron and the guys went to work with chamois and brushes. They also suspected the perpetrators might swing by to admire their handy work, so they hooked up an inch and a half hose line, and loaded it. Sure enough, while they were busy cleaning their truck, these two cops drove slowly by to laugh at the fire guys. But, before they got completely past, one of the firemen grabbed their hose line and made the inside of their patrol car Jacuzzi-like. Once they got out of range these two soaked policemen stopped and got out of their car. With water still running out of their patrol car, they declared war on the firemen. "We'll be back in the morning when you assholes get off duty, and arrest everyone of you sons of bitches on the way home!" Later that night the Captain got their Desk Sergeant on the phone and put an end to this battle before anyone got hurt.

- DOUBLE CROSSES -

Firemen are loyal to each other to a fault when dealin' with outsiders. But, when it comes to fire house pranks on their fire buds, the vulnerable seem to have no friends. The most vulnerable around a fire station, besides the rookie, is anyone who regularly repeats some activity through habit, compulsion, or fun. This rule of thumb especially applies to any fireman who tries to pull off the same prank repeatedly.

THE DOUBLE BUCKET is a simple yet classic example of a fire house double cross. Some two story fire stations develop long standing reputations as *Water Throwin' Houses*. At these stations a fireman can quickly get extremely wet if he loiters too long under a second story window during the summer months. One only has to go upstairs to visualize the ever present danger from above. Screens on key windows will be removed, with a full waste basket or two stationed nearby. By the way, the term *"bucketing"* got its name from the old steel buckets firemen used for this purpose. They have pretty much been replaced with plastic wastepaper baskets to eliminate the problems caused by occasionally dropping one. Unlike a normal job, firemen expect to get wet at work. I mean, moving water from one place to another is one of their basic jobs. Firemen have lotsa uniforms in their lockers, and if all of those get wet, well, there's always their turnout gear.

Anyway, back to our double bucket story. As I explained earlier, repetition equals vulnerability at a fire station. And, the victims of a particular prank often take advantage of any prankster who dares to go to the well too often. This revenge is easily accomplished with a guy above the prankster and some *bait* below. A fireman with a bucket of water on the roof of a two story fire station, has a big advantage on a water thrower on the floor below. But, only if he knows which window he's gonna stick his head out of. Enter the bait. This is generally played by a fireman who is still wet from a prior incident. With such an easy shot loitering below, it won't take long before a second floor water thrower will lean out the appropriate window with bucket in hand. But instead of soakin' the guy below, he quickly goes from prankster to prankee with a direct douche from above.

ROOKIE HANDBALL - I once worked in a multi company fire station across from USC when it had a number of new rookies assigned to each shift. With only a couple of years on the job at the time, I appreciated the instant rise in house seniority and treated *my* new rookies accordingly. Eventually, the rookies were allowed to play handball in the station's court after all their work was done. This handball court had a typical fire station layout. It was a complete concrete enclosure, with the exception of the roof area in the rear. Looking down through this open area was a viewers gallery. It was a firemen built 3 row wooden bleacher affair with stairs coming up from the station's outside yard. I'd had this prank pulled on me about a year earlier and wanted to make sure these rookies didn't miss out on the experience.

As their handball game progressed, preparations were made. An inch and a half hose line with a nozzle was run from a house connection out in the side yard up to the top of the bleacher's stairs, and loaded. With a wedge and a rubber mallet the door into the handball court was quietly 'locked' from the outside. Next came my disguise. I cut a couple of eye holes in a paper towel, drew a happy face on it, and then cut it to fit inside of a breathing apparatus face piece mask that I got off one of the rigs. Next, I grabbed an off-shifter's turnout coat and helmet and headed for the bleachers.

After putting on my gear, I listened as the score of the game got close to the winning point. Then, I slowly poked my head up above the rear wall and looked down on my victims below. At first they didn't quite know what to make of this strange figure peering down from the stands. But, as I raised up higher, exposing the nozzle, they quickly got the picture. After cracking the nozzle to show'em I was serious, I let'em make a break for the locked door before I washed them down the wall and all around the court. Then, just as suddenly as I'd appeared, I disappeared. Dropping the hose line and shedding my disguise as I went, I was down the stairs and back inside the station, and into a seat on the second row in the TV room in a flash. In a bit, a couple of the rookies came in drippin' wet and with loudly *squishin'* tennis shoes trying to identify their tormentor. Naturally, my other fire buds played dumb and seemed generally surprised by their condition. "Hey, I thought you guys were playin' handball, how'd ya get so wet?" Of course their search was fruitless.

A few shifts later the rookies got together for another game. And, as expected, came the usual challenge, "Hibbard, you ain't got a hair on your ass if ya don't get'em again". I agreed and the hook was set. Two more times I pulled the same prank on the same four rookies at the end of their handball games. And, two more times I got off scot-free after playin' water pool with these increasingly angrier young firemen. On my 4th attempt I didn't fare quite so well.

Shortly after the first episode, the rookies figured out how to get out of the locked court. With one boosting another one up, the top guy could reach the top of the shorter rear wall and then pull himself up and into the bleacher area. This, of course, didn't work too well when I was up there with a straight stream flushing'em back down the wall. But, they got so they could get up and out pretty quick after I'd dropped the hose line and left.

My 4th and last attempt started out just like the rest. Right about 'game point' I raised up in the bleacher area in full disguise with nozzle in hand. As soon as they saw me, they charged the rear wall in another vain attempt to crawl out and get their tormentor. Sadistically, I waited until they were right beneath me trying to boost each other up the rear wall before I opened the nozzle to blast'em......but the line immediately went limp! In a panic I dropped the nozzle and ran down the stairs to recharge the line. Then, as I was bent down frantically opening the valve, I got flattened by multiple buckets of water from the second floor. But, that wasn't all. As I was trying to recover from this set back, one of the rookies came charging down the bleacher's stairs with my now charged hose line and chased me back into the station. I can tell ya from experience that that old saying, *"He who laughs last laughs loudest"* has a lot of truth to it.

BEWARE OF OL' JOE - My father told me this classic from the early days of World War II. The Japanese had just recently bombed Pearl Harbor and the west coast was fearful of a possible invasion, or at least some sabotage. As a result, the Los Angeles City Fire Department instigated a 24 hour apparatus floor watch at all of it's fire stations. And, like all fire station floor watches, seniority dictated who got the best and worst time periods. During this period of civil vigilance, a rookie fireman showed up for his first shift at one of the larger downtown fire houses. And, naturally, he promptly got the early AM floor watch period.

As the shifts go by and the rookie starts to get into the fire house routine, one by one his fellow firemen took him aside to warn him about ol' Joe. *"Keep an eye on ol' Joe, sometimes he'll get a little weird on ya"*. When the rookie asked how come nobody's ever complained about him, he got pretty much the same reply of, 'Well he's been one hell of a fireman for all these years and next month he'll have his 30 in and is gonna retire'. Everybody assured him ol' Joe was harmless, but all still suggested that he keep an eye on him! Naturally, the rookie was now watching ol' Joe very closely and tried not to be left alone with him if possible. And then.........

It was a dark and quiet night as this rookie walked his floor watch on a wartime night in L.A. All the fire station's lights had been blacked out and the street outside was empty. His hand held light made eerie shadows on the walls as he walked his beat around the apparatus. Suddenly, there was ol' Joe, leaping out of the darkness and into his path! He was clad in his under shorts and had a fire ax in one hand. His hair was all crazy and toothpaste foam was bubbling out of his mouth as he lunged at the rookie. A lot of runnin' up and down between the apparatus and yellin' followed, with the rookie finally escaping out the station's front door and running off down the street. Back inside, ol' Joe was insisting the laughing firemen go back upstairs and be quiet so he could get the rookie again when he comes back. Meanwhile, the rookie had found an all night business and called the cops about crazy ol' Joe and his ax. "Yeah, yeah", agreed the rookie, "I'll meet ya back in front of the fire station".

As he peered out from the shadows of the station's recessed doors, ol' Joe saw the rookie comin' back down the street. He froze when the rookie paused just before he got to the station. Had ol' Joe been spotted? No, the rookie had just paused to wait for the cops. Just about then, with ol' Joe's attention fixed on his victim, the rookie spotted the cops and an ambulance quietly coming up the street from the other direction. As that 'stupid' rookie again started walking towards the fire station, ol' Joe smiled and forced some more toothpaste foam out of the corners of his mouth. Now at this point, it's important to understand that the whole crew is wide awake and watchin' everything play out below from the darkened 2nd story front windows above.

When the rookie got up to the front of the fire house ol' Joe leaped out of the shadows again with his ax. And then, almost immediately, ol' Joe himself was leaped upon by the cops and a couple of City ambulance attendants. In no time he was wrapped up like a mummy with restraints. Above, the firemen were now all leaning out the windows staring down in disbelief at the turn of events below. With toothpaste foam still drippin' from his chin, ol' Joe tried to explain to the cops that, '*this was all just a big joke*'. The cops paused for a second, considering that possibility. Then, with all his cohorts now leaning out the windows, ol' Joe looked up and pleaded with his fire buds above to straighten all this out. After a long moment of silence one of the captains finally cleared up the issue. "I'm sorry old timer, but I don't think we can cover your ass on this kinda stuff anymore". Ol' Joe, screaming obscenities, was then hustled by both cops and the attendants into the back of the ambulance. They say you could still hear'em yellin' as the ambulance drove off towards the hospital.

- FOLLOW UP -

After the crew finally quit laughing, the Engine Company was 'detailed' over to Central Receiving Hospital to retrieve their 'crazy' Engineer. The Captain quickly smoothed everything over with the two cops and the ambulance attendants with dinner invites on the crew's next shift to rehash the whole story, and laugh at ol' Joe once again. Then, accompanied by his captain and crew, ol' Joe sheepishly was escorted out of his confinement to the laughter of the whole crew on the hospital's graveyard shift.

71

- BATHROOM DANGERS -

In single engine company fire stations the bathroom area is generally just one room consisting of 2 or 3 sinks, a couple of toilets, maybe a urinal, with a shower stall or two. In the multi company fire houses, this area is more likely to be made up of a number of connecting rooms containing a larger number of sinks, toilets & urinals, and showers. The captain's (or captain) quarters have their own appropriately sized separate facilities. These fire station bathroom areas are for the crew's use, and are often very busy places during the period when the shifts are changing. Not surprisingly, the bathroom provides little sanctuary from the fire house pranksters.

THE SURFER - Back in the days when *being a surfer* was becoming a Southern California life style, a young single fireman we'll call Kevin moved down to Manhattan Beach to become part of the surfin' scene. Almost immediately he started returning to the fire station with exciting stories of wild beach parties, sexy beach bunnies, and cool waves. Next he was braggin' about his tan and pointin' out the surfin' knots on his knees. Interesting at first, his fire buds eventually got their fill of his ever increasing 'cool' attitude. One morning while Fireman Kevin was admiring himself in a bathroom mirror, he stepped back and asked the rest of the guys in the room if they didn't think his brown hair was gettin' a little lighter. While Kevin explained to nobody in particular, that a surfer's hair gets blond on the ends from all the sun time, one of his fire buds had an idea.

It seems that one of Kevin's morning rituals was to shake out a little of his liquid hair tonic and vigorously work it into his hair. His particular brand was packaged in a glass bottle, a bottle that the firemen found they could get the shaker cap off easily. During Kevin's next absence an interesting plan was hatched by some of the crew (sometimes it's better to keep your actions between just a few rather than many). One of the guy's wives was a hair dresser and was recruited to come up with some 'Blonding' agent that was about the same color as their surfer's hair tonic.

They started out by just adding a little to his bottle, and had excellent results. After a couple of shifts his hair did get lighter. "Hey guys, my hair IS getting a sun tint", their boy repeated every time he came across a mirror. Naturally the pranksters increased the dose. And, his hair got noticeably blonder. Despite having to suffer through a now even more vainer Fireman Kevin, the rookie hair dressers had to admire their work. Their fire station's resident surfer now actually looked like one. But, now came the fun part. They increased the dose again....Wow! Now, if there is a line somewhere between the look of *cool surfer dude* and *old man of the sea*, their latest mixture definitely crossed it.

The fire guys, were of course, quick to console their buddy; "Oh yeah man, too much sun'll give your hair that yellowing gray look". He finally figured it out, but not quick enough to save himself from having to get a new short haircut, and the attitude adjustment he deserved.

TOILET HOGS - A common problem in a smaller single engine fire station, with a minimum number of toilets, is a member of the crew who repeatedly hogs up a seat. This irritating behavior is most noticeable in the morning hours when firemen's constitutions are more active and regular. But, even in multi company fire stations with plenty of toilets, there is an unexplained urge to screw around with a guy who religiously grabs the sports page and disappears, seemingly forever, into one of the stalls. As usual, there are two basic ways firemen deal with situations like these, directly and indirectly.

Here is an example of the direct method. After the morning coffee drinking and bullshittin' the crew started in on their regular house work. As usual, the guy whose job it was to clean up the bathroom area found one of the toilet stalls still occupied with the same long lingering fireman that seemed to always be in the way of completing his cleaning assignment. While mopping the floor around this irritating obstacle, words were exchanged and he started some direct action to unseat him. With mop in hand, he pushed open the stall door and started mopping around the surprised fireman's feet. One thing led to another, and pretty soon the mop came up off the floor and started to be poked around about face level. Now, at this point, you would probably think that this was gonna pretty much be a one sided confrontation. I mean one guy is fully clothed and standing over his cornered opponent with a dirty wet mop, with the other guy seated, newspaper in hand, and pants down around his ankles. But not so. The fireman on the toilet was indeed cornered, but not unarmed. While fending off the mop attack with one hand, he reached down into the toilet bowl with the other. Grabbing a fresh turd out of the water below,

75

he threw it at his attacker, splattering from head to toe. This immediately drove his tormentor into complete retreat and out of the area.

As the above story should obviously indicate, direct confrontation in matters such as these should generally be avoided. Here are a number of the safer indirect methods that have been used to handle the problem. You can almost always clear a loiterer out of a toilet stall with a sponge and some ammonia. Simply douse the sponge liberally with ammonia and quietly toss it in under the stall. Occasionally, a toilet hog will fight back by kicking the sponge back out. But, this defense can easily be overwhelmed with simply more sponges and more ammonia. *Note: Don't use this method if you're primary goal is to get a seat, since it'll take a while for the ammonia to evaporate so the stall will again be habitable.*

Another effective method to clear a toilet stall is with a garden hose, universal adapter, and some tape. Simply tape one end of the hose to something nearby so it's water stream will arc up, over, and into the targeted stall. Next, using the universal adapter, hook the other end of the hose to a sink faucet. Then, all ya have to do is turn on the cold water as ya quietly leave the room. Hey, isn't that why they put floor drains in those rooms?

At one particular single engine house, which only had two toilet stalls for the crew, the guys tried a little preventive medicine to discourage their irritating toilet hog. The start of every shift was the same. This fireman would fill up on toast & jelly and coffee, grab some pieces of the newspaper, and head for one of the toilet stalls. And that's where he'd stay, forcing all the rest of the guys to take their turns using the other one. Finally, the crew decided to give him a taste of his own medicine.

The next shift started out as usual for their victim; coffee, toast & jelly, grabbed his favorite piece of the newspaper and off to his throne. But, when he went into the bathroom area both of the toilet stalls were full. Irritated, he went out and sat on a bench in the locker room and began to read his paper. A little bit later he went back into the bathroom to see if a spot had opened up. But, he recognized that the same two guys were still in place. He knew they were the same two, because he could clearly see the same worn work boots and denim trousers under one door, and a set of turnout boots and faded turnout pants under the other. "You guys startin' a new career in there?", he mumbled before heading back out to the locker room bench. As the minutes past, pressure was obviously building and discomfort now added to his irritation.

Meanwhile, one of the other crew members had brought in his motorhome and the rest of the crew was using it's toilet while this prank was running it's course. As time went on, our victim forgot about his newspaper and started pacing back and forth in the locker room in front of the bathroom door. As he paced, he made increasingly more derogatory remarks about "those damn toilet hogs". Finally he could stand it no more and charged the stalls demanding to know who the hell these inconsiderate assholes were. When he got no response, he angrily pushed open both doors only to see an empty set of turnouts in one, and only pants & shoes in the other. His normal reaction would be to stomp out into the locker room and confront those damn firemen who were out there laughing at him. But, at that particular moment, he was feeling a much higher calling. So, he simply threw out the empty turnout gear and sat down, while the laughter in the next room continued.

MARBLES - After only a few years on the job, I finagled a transfer out of the Watts area to a large multi company fire house in the suburbs. Shortly after I got there, I got to know the station's two old engineers a little bit better than I really wanted to. The unique responsibilities of the Engineer's position in the fire service produces some truly strange individuals. And, since it's arguably the best job in the station, it also produces a lot of old dudes. Plus, when there's more than one of them in a fire house, they always seem to buddy around together and sometimes get even goofier.

One evening I hit the shower room with only towel in hand and found both of the engineers already in there toweling off. This room was tiled from floor to ceiling and consisted of 4 shower stalls and a small dressing area. While standing outside one stall adjusting the hot water, something made me look back at my new fire buds before I got into the shower. When I did, both of them squatted down in unison and squirted about a dozen marbles out of their collective asses. All of which started bouncing around everywhere on the tiled floor. Coming from a large fire department family, I knew that the best action in a situation like this was no reaction at all. I stepped into the shower and shut the door. As I watched these giggling hydraulic experts through my frosted shower door busily retrieving their marbles, I made a mental note to keep a little closer eye on these two characters.

- THE DORMITORY -

Every fire station has sleeping areas for the whole crew. With the exception of the Captain(s), who have separate quarters, the crew bunks dormitory style. This means one big room with a number of beds. The bigger the fire house, the bigger the room and the larger number of beds. And, if it's above ground level, add a couple of fire poles and their accompanying pole holes. Firemen lay out their bedding on their assigned bed in the evening, and then roll it up and store it in their locker after they get up in the morning. As in a lot of other fire house decisions, choice of beds is determined by 'house seniority'. The choice locations generally seem to be in the corners and away from the locker room doorway.

Dormitory pranks are rarer in single company fire houses for the simple reason that it's too easy to figure out who did it. I mean, with a five man crew, there will only be 4 guys sleeping in the crew's dormitory. But, at a multi company station with say 20 guys on duty, the dormitory can often be an interesting and sometimes scary place after the lights go out. With rare exception, being a firemen is the only job where after a long day at work, instead of going home or off duty, the whole crew eventually sheds their clothes and goes to bed right there at work. In other words, still getting paid while they're sleepin'. This unusual situation creates an atmosphere that produces some very unusual behavior by some so-called normal adults.

I remember one night about 10 an alarm came in for a physical rescue. Everybody jumped up out of bed and spent the next hour gingerly cutting a couple of badly injured people out of a wrecked car. After we returned to the station and went back to bed, a number of the guys returned to what they were doing before they had been so rudely interrupted. That being, lighting farts in the dark to see who could produce the longest 'blue flamer'. The guys with guts enough to remove their under shorts where almost always the winners in these contests, but not without paying an occasional painful price for their competitiveness.

No matter what the hour, there is one certainty in a darkened dormitory with 15 or 20 men in their beds. Not all of them are asleep! Old timers and heavy snorers always seem to be able to fall asleep first, the younger men next, and the rookies generally last. It may be dark and quiet as a fire house can be, but if you're wide awake and bored, there's also probably somebody else in the room that's awake enough to screw with. Many a night I've been laying in bed trying to fall asleep, when someone on the other side of the darkened room would do something to amuse himself and try to keep the rest of us awake. Just about the time you're about to drift off into a peaceful sleep a wind up toy might take off and go zipping across the polished linoleum floor and careening off the walls till it winds down.

At the fire station with the two old engineers it was marbles that seemed to always be rolling forever across the floor at all hours of the night. At one big fire station I worked at everyone took a number of rolls of toilet paper to bed with them. This practice was not for unexpected late night accidents, but rather self protection. It seems that for no particular reason, and at no particular time of night, massive toilet paper fights would break out in the darkness. They seemed to last till everyone was out of ammunition, and then everyone would roll over and go to sleep. Explain that one to your local psychiatrist.

The standard routine of the fire house dormitory is definitely conducive to pre-planned pranks. Let me explain. During the day time hours the dormitory's pretty much unused. The guys dust the floor and straighten up the bed covers, but that's about it. Sometime after dinner the guys start getting their bedding out of their lockers and rolling them out on their beds. Then most of them go back to whatever they were doing. The reason for this earlier bed making practice is so they won't disturb their fellow fire buds who end up going to bed earlier than they do. This way when a fireman is ready to hit the sack, they can simply undress at their locker and quietly go into an already made bed, carrying only their turnout boots & pants. Now I'm sure the devious among you have already recognized the flaw in this routine. Yep, that's right, after leaving your bed completely unattended, you're gonna come back later and get into it in the dark. Obviously, the possibilities for mischief here are endless. Everything from 'short sheeting' a guys *fart sack*, to adding various items of animal, vegetable, and mineral.

Now don't misunderstand, not all dormitory pranks are just crude irritations in the dark. Some require significant preparations before hand and are hilarious to everyone except the victim when they work well. The following is one such example.

81

At a multi company 2-story fire station in downtown L.A., one of the firemen discussed with a number of his fire buds around the kitchen table how he was thinking about gettin' their "new rook" that night. Naturally, egger oners were in ample supply. After the rookie had made up his bed, the pranksters got the big canvas sawdust bag and a bunch of rope off the hook'n'ladder truck and took it up to the dormitory. Then, while one of them kept an eye out for the rookie, the rest laid out an ingenious set up. When done, they shut off the light and left. The rookie stayed up late studying, and they knew the last thing this new kid would do is risk pissin' anybody off by turning on the dormitory lights when he eventually hit the sack.

On this particular night, when the rookie finally closed the books, he found the station strangely quiet. Apparently, most everybody else had already went to bed. In the dormitory, everybody but one lookout was indeed in bed. Most still wide awake and waitin' for their rookie. Pretty soon they got the signal that he was coming up stairs, the lights were turned off and everybody shut up. Eventually the rookie walked in the dormitory and got into his bed as planned.

This station's dormitory was a big rectangular room on the second floor, with a row of beds and a pole hole on each side. The rookie's bed was somewhere in the middle of one of the rows. After the rookie had made up his bed and left, his new fire buds had made sure his top sheet and his blankets were not tucked in before tying a rope to one bottom corner of all of them. They then ran the rope across the room to one of the pole holes and tied it to

82

the heavy sawdust bag. Which was sitting on the front edge of the hole. The rope then continued on, out and around the brass pole, and down the wall to the ringleader's bed. Get the picture? The key to this prank is to have the patience to wait until your victim is half asleep before you pull it off.

Sometimes the wait is too long for a few of the guys and ya start to hear some snoring sounds. But, eventually, the trigger man gives his end of the rope a jerk. This pulls the sawdust bag off the edge of the pole hole, which causes it to go plunging down to the apparatus floor below. And, since it was tied to the rookie's bed covers, his top sheet and blankets immediately go flying off his bed, across the room, and disappearing down the pole hole too. At the same time the ringleader lets go of his end of the rope, and it also goes zipping down the pole hole.

The reaction to this prank is varied, but generally it goes something like this. Shortly after his covers are jerked away he'll sit up in bed, kinda like he's trying to figure out whether or not he's dreamin'. Then, he'll get up and feel around his bed trying to figure out where the hell they went. Next he'll go out to the locker room, get a flashlight, and return to search. At some point, probably while shining his light under some old timer's bed, he'll surely get an angry, "What the hell are you doing?" Eventually, the rookie will go back into the locker room and hunt up another blanket, or finally look down the right pole hole and see where his bedding went.

Some other firemen created obstacles to getting any sleep in a fire station dormitory are snoring, animal calls, talking in their sleep, and nightmares.

A couple of *hunters* assigned to a fire station can easily keep the rest awake with the sounds of all kinds goofy animal calls in the night.

Listening to one of your fire buds talking in his sleep is generally only interesting for a few minutes before somebody will probably try to wake the offender up with some questions about his wife or girlfriend. If that isn't productive or effective, he might get thumped in the head with a roll of toilet paper.

Snoring is an irritating condition that a guy better get use to if he wants to get any sleep around a fire station. Generally, heavy snorers are considerate enough to go to bed later in the evening. Thus allowing the snoring sensitive a chance to get to sleep before the window rattlers retire.

Nightmares, on the other hand, can be real attention getters. On a number of occasions I've been startled awake at work by somebody having an action packed nightmare. Then, after my eyes adjusted to the darkness, I could see that most everybody else in the room was also awake and watchin' one of their crew making a complete fool of himself. Strangely, your closest friends can sometimes be the cruelest people to be around.

- MANAGEMENT -

With the exception of those selected stations that quarter a chief officer, management in a fire house means the Captain. In a semi military organization, like all fire departments are, the Captain holds enormous power over the other firemen assigned to *his* station during their 24 hour shifts. Disobeying a direct order is not tolerated, and you obviously can't get up and go home no matter how pissed off ya get over some supposedly unjust treatment. Thankfully, most fire house captains would aptly fit the description of a benevolent dictator. Even the ornery ones know the truth in that old saying, *"A captain who takes care of his crew, is more apt to have a crew that will take care of him"*. The latter is important, because a disloyal crew can easily make a bad captain look incompetent.

When it comes to fire house pranks the captain is generally off limits. The reason for this is that the captain can easily get even in a most official way. I've been at fire stations where somebody was stupid enough to bucket a captain. The common result, after their leader changes into a dry uniform, is that the whole crew is told to, "saddle up guys, we're going out for a little drill." After a couple of hours of laying out hundreds of feet of hose and squirtin' water around some empty parking lot, most crews will likely get the message. At the same time, a captain will generally turn a blind eye to most other fire house pranks among his crew. Of course, there are exceptions to all of this.

Considering a captain's unique position, the only *safe* fire house prank that can be played on a captain is one where the members of the crew do not appear to be responsible. This is tough, since they are generally the only other ones there. Tough, but not impossible.

TOILET GHOST - Fireman Frank worked at a two story fire station in downtown L.A. The single engine company's fire truck was parked on a ground level apparatus floor, with most everything else being upstairs. Up on the second floor, the crew's quarters was in the rear of the building and the captain's was up front. Back in the days when 'the rules' weren't so restrictive, it wasn't unusual to have a fireman that was assigned to that station sleepin' in the dormitory on his shifts off. Whatever the reason for a fellas temporary lack of lodging, a brother fireman was always welcome as long as he didn't become a pain in the ass to the crew on duty.

Fireman Frank was not a pain in the ass, but rather an asset whether on duty or not. Before becoming a fireman, Frank was a plumber by trade. And, when he heard one shift repeatedly complaining about the trouble they were having with their shift's hard assed captain, he volunteered his services. Working only when the Company was out of the fire station taking care of business in their district, he ran a long strand of steel wire from the crew's dormitory up to the pipe closet behind the captain's bathroom. This was no small effort. It went up into the attic crawl space, and using small caged pulleys, then ran inconspicuously down into the pipe closet. Next, he re-plumbed and jury rigged the valve set up so the captain's toilet could be flushed by either a captain in their bathroom or by pulling on a wire in the crew's dormitory.

The key to this prank was keeping the guys on the other two shifts from pullin' that wire on their own captains. It's hard enough convincing one captain that he's goin' nuts, let alone three. After "Frank's Flusher" was completed, the firemen on the C-shift *flushed* their skipper at midnight and then again at three AM. Being only a door away from the captain's bed, a noisy toilet flushing in the middle of the night must have been a little unnerving, even for the C-shift's fearless leader. The next morning the Captain told his 'toilet story' to whoever would listen, and the on-coming Captain assured him he'd call a City plumber if it continued. The next shift, when told that their toilet worked just fine during his absence. At that point, this captain must have at least considered the possibility that maybe he was actually dreaming.

On that shift his crew got him again with three flushes, all in the wee hours. After the last one, about 4 AM, the Captain was up with flashlight in hand and peering around in the pipe closet located behind his shitter. But, since this captain was a little more familiar with the books than plumbing repair, he found no obvious reason for the mysterious midnight flushings. When he returned to spend his third night with the 'Toilet Ghost', the first thing he did when he went on duty was put in a call for a City plumber.

Now remember, at this point nobody but the C-shift Captain had heard the captain's toilet flush on its own. And, members on all the shifts, including the other two captains, had now started making *toilet remarks* in his presence. And also, seriously asking the C-shift Captain some irritating dead pan questions like: "Hey Cap, did ya ever have this kinda problem before ?" "Why do ya think the 'Toilet Ghost' is only pickin' on you, Skipper?" "Are ya sure it's the toilet?" And so on.

Naturally, the crew posted a watch in the side yard, and intercepted the City plumber as soon as he and his City truck pulled in. Firemen traditionally maintain a good relationship with City workers of all kinds, but especially those craftsmen who maintain their fire houses, i.e., electricians, cabinet men, plumbers, heating & air conditioning guys, etc. The firemen often treat these guys especially nice, inviting'em in for lunch and sometimes including'em in the fire house goings on. That would also include fire house pranks, which occasionally turn out to be on them.

After a quick briefing, the plumber enthusiastically counted himself in on the prank and headed for the front office to hunt up the Captain. After hearing the Captain retell his toilet story for about the umpteenth time, the plumber went straight to work after the Captain let him into the pipe closet. The Captain stood watching him through the narrow doorway for awhile. But, finally got his fill of the plumber's blasting portable radio and went to join the rest of his crew in the kitchen. After a bit, the plumber wandered into the kitchen and gave the Captain the worst news possible, "Everything's OK!"

The Captain irritatingly started to repeat his story again while insisting that "something must be causing it!" The plumber went on about valves and pressure regulator settings and how it was flushin' just fine. And then, finished up his report by jokingly askin' the Captain if he's sure he hadn't just been dreaming? This didn't set well with their skipper, as he abruptly got up from the table and stomped off to his office. Then, partly out of cruelty, and partly just to show the plumber that "Frank's Flusher" really worked, they sent the rookie back to the dormitory to pull on the wire. In just a very few moments the Captain burst back into the kitchen still fastening up his pants and yellin' for the plumber to follow him. In an amazing stroke of fire house luck, this daytime flush had obviously caught their captain sittin' on it! The immediate effect was that the plumber got to goof off for another hour in the pipe closet checkin' things out, and the crew once again got to laugh their asses off when their captain left the room.

Sadly, this excellent prank came to an anti-climactic ending. With the *Toilet Ghost* continuing its nightly visits, the Captain started staying up a lot later at night and trying to catch some sleep in the TV chairs. Consequently, on some shifts the fireman in charge of pullin' the wire would fall asleep long before the Captain would retire to his quarters. And finally, Frank, who was living at the station, felt he had to return the station's plumbing to normal before he packed up his stuff and finally moved back in with his wife. I'm not sure the C-shift Captain ever found out who was behind the Toilet Ghost.

CHIEF'S PHONE - This Battalion Chief was a large, loud, and egotistical individual with one of those fold-over hairdos. One of those supervisors that always had to be the center of any kitchen table conversation, but never let ya forget he was in charge. In other words, a real pain in the ass to live with in a small fire station. He wanted to be let in on all the fire house pranks, but made it clear he was not to be screwed around with.

One time he was walking across the apparatus floor right next to the fire truck, while one of the engineers was busy up in the hose bed of his rig working with an air hose. This chief grew what was left of his blond hair really long on one side and then carefully combed it up and over his shinning bald spot every morning. As he past by, the Engineer just couldn't resist the opportunity to give the chief's fragile hairdo a supposedly innocent blast of compressed air. This rearrangement immediately gave the Chief a stupid 'Ben Franklin look' on one side, and had everybody in the vicinity laughing at him. This was a mistake, since during the subsequent shifts this chief made the Engineer pay dearly for his foolish action in a variety of official ways.

At this station, the chief's quarters was pretty much the same as the Captain's, that being a bedroom and bathroom area. And, just like the fire station's front office, both the Captain and the Chief had the same set of two phones in their quarters. One would be a standard dial phone connected to the City business lines, and the other one being the "Fire Phone". The latter known as *the red phone*, since most of them are, connects whoever picks it up directly to the Department's dispatchers. From the other end of the line, a dispatcher can ring up the chief's phone or the captain's separately. This set up allows the Chief to receive and respond to an alarm at night without gettin' the whole fire station up if they are not also being dispatched.

One day the crew was coffeeing up in the kitchen with one of their favorite City repairmen. This guy was out at the fire station that shift to 'work on the phones'. During the chatter somebody remarked, "we could sure drive the Chief nuts if only we could ring his fire phone from in here".
"I can do that", bragged the phone guy.

The repairman's coffee cup was quickly freshened up and the fire guys all slid up a little closer. Then, after agreeing to keep this just among themselves, they went to work. After the firemen drilled a few key holes in the walls, ran a couple of wires from inside a kitchen cabinet, through a couple of rooms, and into the back of the main communications panel, the phone guy made the connections. And sure enough, when ya touched the two wires together in the kitchen cabinet, the chief's fire phone rang on his bedside night stand just like it was a real call.

Just like the *toilet flushers* in the previous story, the *phone ringers* in this prank only picked on one particular victim. The two other battalion chiefs that worked on the other shifts in the station experienced no communications problems at all. But, sometimes late at night, they say you could often hear their grumpy old Chief bellowing into his fire phone. "Bullshit, the goddamn phone just rang!"

Sometimes he'd really be givin' them hell, "I don't know what kinda clowns you got down there, but I'm gonna have somebody's ass if this crap don't stop". At one point he even got up out of bed and went down there to chew on those dispatchers in person. Naturally, these poor guys didn't have a clue on what the hell this strange looking chief was talking about. I say strange, because he always looked a little 'slouchy'. But, when forced to get up late at night he really complimented that look when a lot of that long blond hair, from his collapsing *fold-over*, would generally be stickin' awkwardly out from under just one side of his hat. Nobody sarcastically asked this guy if he'd *'just been dreamin'*.

Also like the *toilet flushers*, this prank also had an anti-climatic ending for basically the same reason. After a couple of weeks of agitating an already unpleasant individual, the phone repair guy returned. "Hey guys, that chief of yours has stirred up so much shit down at Communications that my boss is threatening to come out here and look into the *problem* himself. And so, the wires were removed. But, not before somebody made a note of which terminals they were connected to. I mean, that's the kinda info ya never know when ya might need again.

INFIDELITY - One of Captain Smith's first assignments as a new captain was a relatively quiet single engine house out in the suburbs of L.A. But, as a young go getter rapidly working his way up through the ranks, Captain Smith would've clearly rather had a busier assignment. It became clear to his crew almost immediately that the activity level around their sleepy neighborhood fire station was gonna go way up. Captain Smith was an all right guy, but like an overactive kid during nap time, he was often a pain in the ass. Additionally, Captain Smith was just a kid compared to most of his crew. Thoroughly schooled in the manuals, this young man was still relatively wet behind the ears as far as *real* life experience was concerned. After quite a few months of this new heightened station activity, their new leader suddenly seemed to easily get side tracked from keepin' the crew busy. This, by an increasing number of visits by a young lady he never introduced. One night, after this pattern had continued for about a month, he finally confessed to the crew he was havin' an affair. Duh!

This must of been a real mind twister for this guy, as he subsequently disclosed he'd married his sweetheart right out of high school and had never been with another woman up until now. Naturally, a grinning crew had lotsa suggestions on how to handle the pros and cons of his exciting situation. As the weeks went by, the Captain obviously felt some relief being able to vent his emotions to the fire guys. On one hand he loved his wife and felt guilty as hell about what he was doing. On the other, he loved the sex. But finally, after getting tired of repeatedly having to listen to the latest episode of this on going battle within himself, his fire buds decided to give their perplexed captain a little push towards making a decision.

I think they sell'em at pool supply and joke stores. You know, those harmless little pills that turns your urine a bright orange. I think they're sold to help ya train your kids not to pee in the pool. Well, on one shift the crew ground up a few of these pills and made sure they ended up in the captain's food at lunch. That night they all sat around quietly listening in the TV room while

93

their captain was up in the front office going over his paperwork. Finally, they heard him yell out in shock. One of the crew quickly went up to check on their skipper, and found the Captain still standing over his toilet bowl. "Ya OK, Cap?"

"I don't know", mumbled the Captain, seemingly on stun with his fly still open. This was nothing he could hide, since when he recoiled at the sight, he had sprayed bright orange pee trails all over the white porcelain.

"Jesus, Cap, maybe you better lie down", exclaimed the fireman when he got up close enough to see the full extent the Captain's apparent problem. "Front office, front office" he yelled out, to alert the rest of the crew. And, in no time, the Captain's bedroom was completely full of hand wringers.

"Oh shit", whispered one member of the crew just loud enough for the Captain to over hear, "my brother got something like that over in Vietnam and almost had to have his penis cut off". The Captain groaned and sat down on his bed. He was hooked.

One of the guys, who everyone knew had paramedic training, said that he had some penicillin which might knock it if he'd just recently caught it. The Captain was beside himself. "What am I going to tell my wife?", he moaned. The guys smiled behind his back as they assured him everything was gonna be all right. Then they steered him back into the kitchen where the guy said he had the pills, and where it was much more comfortable for all of them to enjoy their captain's new ailment. Once there, the Captain gulped down a handful of penicillin (actually vitamin C).

The next morning the captain's urine had pretty much returned to its normal color, but he still had that 'whoa is me' look on his face when he finally left for home. Then, in a completely unexpected turn of events, his wife had picked that particular morning to confront her husband with her suspicions. As soon as he walked in the front door his wife yelled at him, "You've been with another woman!" Apparently already in a weakened mental state after his hectic day at the fire station, this foolish philanderer immediately broke down and confessed his whole affair. But wisely, since he knew he wasn't gonna be sleepin' with her anytime in the foreseeable future, he figured the orange piss part of the story could wait 'till later.

- ROOKIES -

Fire departments everywhere have one thing in common, something that is missing in almost every other job. That is, its members eat, sleep, and repeatedly put their asses on the line at a moments notice....*Together!* This produces a special relationship between firemen in fire houses all across this country. A new rookie fireman is an untested outsider when he is first hired by a fire department. Sure, he's been through a training course, but that's nothing compared to the reality of engine house life and the thrill of the unknown waiting at the end of every emergency run.

There are a few down sides for a rookie in his brand new exciting job. You see, most fire departments of any size have one year probationary periods for new rookie fireman. In other words, a rookie fireman has one year to prove that he can and will carry his load, or lose his great new job. And, they also must prove that they can get along with the guys in the station by controlling both their mouth and their emotions. This is not all that easy, since a lot of a rookie's new friends are trying to get a rise out of him every chance they get. A rookie gets to clean the toilets, and all the other disagreeable jobs no matter what station he works at during his first year.

Rookies also get to be last in most everything, except when it comes to some of the more grizzly aspects of some emergency situations. But more importantly, the arrival of a brand new rookie will give any latent fire house prankster a brand new lease on life. And, not surprisingly, some of the most active rookie tormentors are those guys who got heavily harassed during their rookie year. You'll notice that there are rookie stories scattered throughout this book, and here are a few more descriptions the obstacles rookies may have to deal with on their way to becoming an accepted member of the Fire Department.

Trying to gross out a rookie at meal time is not unusual. Picture a rookie sitting down last at the kitchen table for the crew's noon meal. A table where the food has already been evenly proportioned out into the required number of plates. As soon as he slips down into his seat on the bench between two other hungry firemen, he sees that *his* polish sausage looks a little different than everyone else's. At this point, the rookie starts to comprehend that instead of a sausage, his is a nicely shaped human turd sharing the plate with his Chile beans. "What's wrong", demands the fireman across the table, "ain't ya gonna eat yours?" Without really waiting a for a response, he reaches across with his plate and fork and mashes the turd in two. Then, slides about half of it off the rookie's plate onto his. This maneuver, along with the terrible smell it released, caused the gagging rookie to make a serious move towards the sink.

There are, of course, a number of possible versions of the preceding example. Some too gross to describe in this book. But, one fireman's ingenious use of bacon for this purpose does deserve mention. Picture a similar kitchen table scene as described above, but with everything going along just fine about half way through the meal. Good food, good fellowship, this particular rookie was enjoyin' life as a new fireman. Little did he know that the fireman across the table from him had a *bacon string* up his nose. A bacon string is that thin gooey string of white fat that runs throughout uncooked bacon. It seems this fireman separated out a piece of this stringy fat, and just before he sat down for dinner, shoved it up inside one of his nostrils. Then, when the time was right, and he had the rookie's attention, he started complaining about a problem his was havin' with his nose. "Been bothering me all day", he said, as he kinda rubbed one side of it. And then to the astonishment of the wide eyed rookie, he slowly pulls this long string of gooey white something out of his nose and holds it up by one end for inspection. The shocked expression on the rookie's face was nothing compared to the look he got when this 'booger eater' suddenly put one end of it in his mouth and sucked it up like a limp piece of spaghetti. This rookie was also soon gagging at the sink amid the laughter of the whole crew.

The first year for a rookie is a 12 month test on whether or not he's a regular guy and someone who can be trusted in a pinch. On most fire departments, a new rookie is transferred around to two or three fire stations during his probationary period. This is probably to get the input from a larger number of captains. Or, maybe just to give more firemen a chance to screw with him. Whatever the reason, a new rookie will run into a lot of new *friends* during his first year. And, to describe some of them as real characters would be to understate their occasional aberrant behavior. The fire service is noted for bringing out this strangeness in some of its members.

Rookies are tormented both directly and indirectly, and the amount of *testing* each individual rookie receives is determined by the crew, according to how well he reacts to the standard harassment. Like a bunch of chickens pickin' on the weak one, if somebody stumbles onto something that really bothers a new rookie it might be a long year for him. As an example, religious nuts who can't stand profanity, or using the Lord's name in vain, are likely to be purposely and repeatedly exposed to some things that would make a whore blush. Modesty is always considered a weakness. And, there's always some guy in the locker room who wants to know if the rookie's got any nude pictures of his wife or girl friend. While proudly showin' the rookie naked pictures of his. Plus, there's these problems.

After a rookie has made up his bed in the dormitory, somebody cuts up some of the stiff bristles off a scrub brush and sprinkles these small pieces in his bed. Unnoticed when he crawls into his fart sack, he'll spend that night flippin' and floppin', and itchin' and scratchin' until the morning light reveals the reason.

Invariably, whenever the guys find a rookie who is a little on the naive and shy side, he'll eventually run into some grizzly old timer who'll try to slide into bed with him after the lights have gone out in the dormitory. A rookie's reaction to this is often very telling on how he'll react in other serious situations.

Most every fire station has a tall and generally enclosed hose tower which wet hose lines are hoisted up into to dry before they are reused. All of these towers are equipped with a rope and pulley set up to hoist up the hose, and a long ladder up to a platform so a fireman can go aloft to hook each hose up at the top, and then send the hook back down for the next one. Rookies are almost always the ones who are sent up the ladder to the top of the tower. And, almost every rookie, during his first year, will find out what a vulnerable position the top of the hose tower can be.

 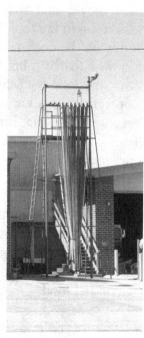

-HOSE TOWERS. An enclosed hose tower (on the left) is located at the rear corner of this 2-story fire station. The structure on the right of it is the station's handball court. An open hose tower (pictured on the right) is often seen in the drier southwestern parts of the country were rain is seldom a problem. Owls for the rookies to feed generally roost in the enclosed version.-

Now obviously, it's easy to get the rookie up into the hose tower when the crew is out washing and hanging up wet hose. But that's not the only way to get him aloft. It's not unusual, on some night at his first fire station, for the rookie to be asked to 'feed the owl'. When they get that expected blank look, the crew will explain to there rookie that they've got a semi tame owl that has been roostin' up in the top of their hose tower for quite some time now. And, with the cook handing him some leftovers from dinner, he's informed that it's his turn to climb up into the top of the hose tower and feed it. Maybe not really believing them, but eager to cooperate, the rookie dutifully goes out and climbs up the ladder. Once up on the platform in top of the tower he finds no evidence of any owl, but does began to hear the noise of water below as the rope and pulley start moving. In preparation of their prank, the crew had connected up an inch hand line with a spray nozzle in the adjoining outside yard, and loaded it. Then, as soon as the rookie got up to the top of the tower, they opened up the nozzle and started hauling it up towards him. From personal experience I can attest that this prank produces a very wet and helpless feeling, as this blasting nozzle quickly climbs up towards you and your small sack of owl food.

Picture you're a new firefighter spending one of your first few nights at the fire house. When you finally go to bed, you carefully place your new turnout boots & pants at the side of your bed before you crawl in. Fully expecting them to be just as you left them if ya have to get up in a hurry. Then, sometime during the night, your turnouts are silently spirited away and into the locker room for some changes. The rookie's turnout pants are replaced with a pair of turnout pants that have had the legs cut off really short. And then, his boots & new pants are quietly returned to the rookie's bedside. If everything goes right, an alarm will come in before the morning comes. When it does, the fun begins.

The bright lights snap on and a loud gong or bell immediately wakes everybody up in the dormitory. Thousands of times a night, all across our country, night alarms like this initiate the same routine among firemen on duty. They sit up in bed, swing their legs over the side and slip their feet down into their turnout boots. From that point, it's simply a matter of standing up, pullin' up your pants, and start heading for your fire truck. It's somewhere about here that the rookie with the funny pants will recognize that he has a problem. But there's not much he can do about it right then, since failure to get aboard the rig when an alarm comes in is an unforgivable sin in the fire service.

How long they let the rookie suffer through the indignity of his silly looking outfit is generally determined by the nature of their call. If they're headed for a structure fire, somebody will probably toss him his full length pants so he can change into them in route. If on the other hand, they're responding to a rubbish fire or the like, the guys just might just let their rookie do his thing when they get on scene. And then loudly explain to any curious onlookers, "Oh yeah....he's kinda new on the job".

Now of course, a rookie can get all puffed up and tell his new fire buds to kiss his ass, but that's a no win situation no matter what the outcome. A rookie knows from the git that if he can keep his cool and survive that first year, he'll become one of the guys and can look forward to many more years of havin' one of the best jobs in the world.

And finally, here's a personal story of an unusual rookie tradition they practice on the Pasadena Fire Department. It was the last shift of the calendar year and I was a rookie fireman working at Fire Station #4 on the west side of town. Sometime after dinner I was called to the front office and told by the Captain that I was being 'detailed' over to Headquarters for the remainder of the shift.

Fire Station #1 occupied the first two floors of a multi story building in downtown Pasadena, with the Department's Business Offices on the floors above. As soon as I got there, I found one of the captains in the front office and checked in. "Store your gear and look around a bit, then hunt me up in the kitchen and I'll explain your assignment tonight". Now, this captain didn't laugh or anything, but I could sense that he found something humorous about my arrival. After bringing in my gear and looking over the fire trucks, I went upstairs to the kitchen.

It was New Year's Eve and downtown Pasadena was alive with pre-parade activity. This Headquarters Station was no exception, with lots of City Officials and policemen moving about. The Kitchen was the hub of all this activity with a number of different conversations going on around the two long tables. As soon as I walked in, the Captain I'd spoke to earlier motioned me over and introduced me to the other firemen he was sitting with. And then, in a voice loud enough so everybody in the kitchen could hear, said, *"Fireman Hibbard here is gonna be on **Parade Patrol** tonight"*. I immediately became the center of attention in the room, as some laughed and others just shook their heads. "Listen Kid", the Captain continued on, "it ain't all that bad, I mean you're gonna have two cops with ya". Trying not to look too concerned, I jokingly asked him if a title went with this job. "Well", he said smiling, "by morning you'll probably the most hated guy in town". Amid the laughter, the Captain assigned another fireman to check me out on their Patrol rig and to explain the routine.

The Patrol rig was a big red pick up truck complete with red lights, fire radio, and siren. It also had a water tank, a pump, and about a hundred feet of preconnected 1" hose. It was about 10 PM, and my assignment for the rest of the shift was to put out all the camp fires along the parade route.....and, keep'em out! Now this may not seem like such a big deal on the surface, but on this December 31st evening it dipped to well below freezing in Pasadena. And, literally hundreds and hundreds of people were streaming into town to stake out front row spots along Colorado Boulevard for the next morning's parade. These folks were carrying everything imaginable to make their overnight curbside stay enjoyable, including firewood and alcohol. But, the City decided long ago that it would not allow the crowd to build fires along the parade route (small barbecues were OK) for fear of embers igniting the roofs of nearby businesses. Are ya starting to get the picture here? For the rest of the night this rookie fireman was gonna be the *'evil fire grinch'* who's official job was to steal the warmth from a lot of Pasadena's alcohol impaired visitors.

The first pass wasn't too bad, as most of the fires were those of family groups who were willing to listen to reason and cooperate. Others were not so receptive, but I was able to put all the fires out with a minimum of water and disturbance to both the violator's camp and the other gutter dwellers immediately down stream. My next run down the parade route was shortly after midnight and I encountered a number of the same fires I had extinguished earlier, plus some new ones. Also, the attitudes of the fire owners were much worse than before. It was also colder. Around 2 or 3 in the morning the tone of the crowd has really changed. The street football and volley ball games had pretty much broken up and most responsible folks were tightly bundled up in sleeping bags trying to catch some sleep or ward off the cold. But, there still was some activity along the parade route by the die-hards who had more liquor and firewood than warm clothing.

Things did not go well on this trip. The first fire I came to was one I had already put out twice before. And, my police escort had gradually taken to following me from an increasing distance. Maybe these two cops weren't joking when they laughingly said they'd win $20 in the pool if I got punched on this run. After stopping just past this first fire, I was confronted by 3 men as I started to pull the hose out of the back of the truck.

"You Jerk", one of them yelled out.

"Hey, I'm just following orders", I unemotionally mumbled as I started towards their fire.

Then, just before I was able to wet it down, one of these irate partyers shut the valve off at the truck. This embarrassing standoff ended when my *Helpers* finally pulled up and turned their flashing lights on. Thankfully, there were no confrontations at the next three fires, but I was thoroughly and loudly denounced as the devil himself while I was dousing their fires. At one fire, an elderly lady actually called me an "evil piece of shit". My two cop escorts seemed to see a lot of humor in this, as I could see them laughing inside of their warm police car.

There were only two guys warming themselves at the next fire I came upon. Both were wearing shorts and loudly sharing a quart bottle of something brown. When I stopped and got the hose out, I was aggressively confronted by these two gentlemen who claimed that they'd stick my hose up were the sun don't shine if I didn't get the hell out of there. When I didn't retreat fast enough, one guy menacingly reached out and grabbed for the nozzle I was holding. In as much surprise as defense, I pulled the nozzle open full blast for what seemed like only a second, and then shut it off. At that point, everything seemed to stand still for the longest moment.

I can still clearly remember both of them, standing there dripping wet, trying to comprehend what had just happened. But then things started moving again, and they were yelling and moving towards me. I cracked the nozzle open a little and started backing up towards the truck. Luckily, the cops finally pulled up and blasted their siren to break up this pending ass kickin'. As the cops were sternly informing these two wet and now freezing parade fans that they couldn't beat up the fireman, I soaked their fire down big time. After that incident, along with my hollow threat to return to the station for more help, my helpers started staying right up behind me and turned on their flashing lights every time I stopped at another fire. The rest of the shift was tense, but pretty much violence free.

- MISCELLANEOUS DEVIOUSNESS -

Here are a varied grab bag of fire house pranks that also need to be retold:

The New Car - Firemen are notoriously 'nice car people', as a lot of their spare time around the fire station is spent cleaning and maintaining their personal vehicles. So naturally, when a fire station member buys a brand new car it's the center of attention in the side yard for a number of shifts. "How's it run?" "What kinda mileage do ya get?" "What's this do?", are the kind of questions the new buyer will be inundated with from his fire buds.

Every so often ya get a new car buyer that is a real nut on his new car and its gas mileage. When that happens, it's not unusual for the guys at work to start addin' a little gas to his tank every shift. The next thing ya know, he'll be braggin' his ass off around the kitchen table about how great a mileage he's getting. "Oh yeah, it's getting better every time I check it!" The guys will keep up the additions for a week or so, and then start siphoning a little bit out every shift.

Sometime later, this new car owner will not quite be so perky about his *amazing* mileage anymore. In fact, when questioned about it by his fire buds, he'll probably more than likely be a little pissed off about it. Pretty soon the guys will start suggesting that he take his pride and joy back to the dealer.

"You know, they got a lemon law, don't ya?"

"Oh yeah, they gotta fix something like that". And, so it goes, as the guys milk this new car owner's gullibility for all it's worth.

Quarter in the Funnel - When the intended victim walks into the kitchen he sees his fire buds busily involved in some kind of an apparent game of skill. As he watches, while getting himself a fresh cup of coffee, he sees that the guys are taking turns trying to get a quarter to drop off their foreheads and into a funnel stuck into their pants behind their belt buckle. The funnel is about 4 or 5 inches across, but not so big as to let the quarter pass all the way through its spout.

Pretty soon, after watching his fire buds taking their turns, of course, he wants to try it. The next thing he knows he's standing up with his head arched back and the funnel stuck down the front of his pants. One fireman then carefully places the quarter on his forehead and steps back. Then, while the victim is busy concentrating on the quarter, one of his other fire buds casually pours a cup of cold coffee into the funnel!

Car Washer - Remember the story of the habitual car washer verses the water throwers that I detailed earlier? Well, a more covert method of dealing with this type of irritation is bird seed or popcorn. Coming out to see your meticulously washed and chamiosed car now hosting a large congregation of neighborhood birds is definitely an attention getter.

Hot Seat - Some fire stations are known for one particular prank that the crew repeatedly pulls on newcomers. They obviously have to concentrate on strangers because most everybody involved with that station will have already been cut in to it. One of these is a "Hot Seat".

110

Most fire house kitchens contain one or two long wooden tables, along with sturdy wooden benches. A hot seat is easily built into one of these benches with an old Ford coil. These old coils have the unique ability to store a charge of electricity for a long time. The coil is mounted underneath the bench. Then, a tiny hole is drilled down through the sitting surface of the bench. Now, when the hot wire from the coil is carefully run up through the hole to just below the surface above, and the coil is given a charge......this prank becomes cocked, ready, and waitin' for anybody foolish enough to sit down on that spot on the bench.

Often a button is wired into the system so a fireman at the other end of the bench can jolt the person sitting in the hot seat when the time is just right. This is generally when the victim is doing something like sipping his coffee, or maybe when you're simply tried of listening to some bullshit story he's tellin' the guys. At the right time, the fireman at the other end of the bench would push the button and send about a zillion harmless volts through the guy's ass. I think this is maybe where that old saying, *"I Really got a rise out of him"*, came from. Occasionally you'll get some real sick individuals on the button, who specialize in gettin' their victims to straddle the wire before zappin'em.

Sparky - Even the fire house mascot is not exempt from getting caught up in an occasional fire station prank. Sparky was Fire Station 103's loyal mascot, one of the few Dalmatians on the L.A. City Fire Department at the time. Like all male dogs, Sparky just loved to check out the tires of all the firemen's private vehicles when they were parked at the station. And, of course, marking'em with a little squirt of his own.

After getting some fancy new chrome wheels for his truck, Fireman Carl vowed to his fire buds that he was gonna train Sparky not to piss on his new rims. Naturally, the guys watched Carl's dog training methods with interest. Fireman Carl would check the wheels on his truck periodically during the shift, and when he found Sparky had peed on one of them a training session would begin. He'd gather up a bucket of water, a chamois, and Sparky's leash. Then he'd give old Sparky a call. When the dog showed up, on would go his leash and off to the soiled wheel they'd go. Once there, Sparky would be tied close by while the *Dog Trainer* simultaneously cleaned off his wheel and thoroughly chewed his ass. Then, he'd pour the remaining water in his bucket on the dog and leave him sittin' out there soakin' wet to think about it for a while.

As the fire guys watched this unusual method unfold, after a number of shifts they actually started to see some results. Sparky started skipping Fireman Carl's truck when making his rounds through the parking lot. This would have been the end of the story, except now Fireman Carl suddenly became a vocally irritating self proclaimed dog training expert. But....only for awhile. Somebody on the crew soon discovered that a splash of coffee on a chrome rim looks a whole lot like dog piss. And, even though Sparky was now giving Carl's truck a wide berth, a couple of Sparky's fire buds started fillin' in for him.

This quickly had the desired effect on the Dog Trainer, as he noticeably toned down his boastin' about his dog training expertise. But, a blameless Sparky now went back to the lease & bucket routine every time Fireman Carl found some coffee on one of his wheels. This set up was fun for awhile, but eventually the guys started feeling sorry for Sparky and started pushing it to the absurd. When they started this prank it was just a small splash of coffee on one wheel at a time. Now they went to two wheels at a time, then three, and finally all four before ol' Carl knew he'd been had. Sparky, of course, came out of this prank none the worse for wear. But, for a while, he was surely the cleanest Fire Dog in the vicinity.

The Cook - Generally speaking, every shift, everybody on the crew will kick in a few bucks each to be counted in for both a lunch and dinner meal while on duty. Basically, there are two ways to handle the cooking chores at the fire station. One is for <u>all</u> the members to take a turn at being the *Cook*. The other choice is to find a *permanent cook* on your crew who'll handle the cooking chores every shift. Whatever the arrangement decided on, the rest of the guys on the shift regularly handle the Cook's normal fire house duties so he can concentrate on whippin' up two meals that are up to fire house standards. Lunch and dinner are always two of the more important activities every shift at any fire house.

A good permanent fire house cook on a crew is a valuable asset to the shift and is rarely screwed around with for obvious reasons. But, with regard to one fire house tradition, even he is not exempt.

Desert is a regular and expected part of every dinner meal. Ice cream is the norm, but often the cook will bake a cake or the like for his fire buds. Naturally, those kind of items are extremely vulnerable to *'samplers'* who are almost always moving in and out of the kitchen while these freshly baked goods are cooling and waiting for after dinner. And therefore, cooks will go out of their way to keep their creations for being violated until their time. On the other hand, *coring the cake* is a traditional fire station prank that over rules any cook's seniority or privilege.

Be it a luscious double layer chocolate, or a large one layer with vanilla frosting and a message on top, a plug or two will surely get cut out of the center of it before the dinner call. Some cooks get really furious when this happens. But apparently, it's just something firemen have to do.

When everyone on the shift takes a turn at cookin', pranks on the Cook are not all that uncommon. But, they're a little tricky. I mean, sometimes it's tough to screw around with the Cook without screwing up the food.....your food! Enter food coloring. I can attest that fire station mashed potatoes can come in a wide variety of colors. This also goes for gravy and sauces of all kinds. Vegetables also turn some interesting colors when you add a little color to the water ya cook'em in.

This type of dinner time activities is not always a one way street. Sometimes a cook will get a little tired of the harassment and fight back. Imagine how much fun a cook can have by simply throwing in a few pieces of stewing chicken with the bunch of frying chicken he's gonna cook up in the oven. At dinner time, the regular frying chicken is cooked just right and ready to eat. While those identical looking pieces of stewing chicken are still so tough you can't even cut off a piece, much less chew it.

- THE SHOOTING -

Back in the early '60s, three men at Fire Station 45 pulled off one of LAFD's best pranks ever.

45's consisted of a single engine company along with a smaller truck called a Booster Tank. Each shift had a captain, an engineer, and 5 firemen, one of which was a rookie. Unlike most fire house pranks, the Captain was the ring leader on this one. One fireman on his crew was quite a character known as 'Curly'. He was sort of a big county type with long curly hair. He also had a fiery temper, was sorta a gun nut, and only marginally accepted authority. Other than that, he was a respected fire fighter and always fun to be around. One shift the guys again started kiddin' Fireman Curly about the excessive length of his hair, with one of them finally suggesting that maybe "we oughta get him down and cut it for him".

To that suggestion, Curly said, "there ain't nearly enough of you assholes to cut my hair!" Although his challenge went unanswered at the time, it was definitely not forgotten.

The Captain was a prankster from the old school and not about to let Curly's challenge go to waste. If the crew wasn't gonna jump on him and cut his hair, why not turn the whole thing around on the crew? He quietly shared his idea with Fireman Mel, another established station house *'turd stirrer'*, who liked it. Then, they both approached Curly with the idea. Their plan was to stage his forced hair cutting. Then, mad as hell, Curly would go get a gun and come back and shoot Fireman Mel. "Oh yeah, that sounds great", agreed Fireman Curly almost too quickly. The three of them then planned out the details of their prank.

On their next shift this trio put their plan into action. After the regular morning chores had been completed, the Captain had everybody gather out in the parking lot under the pretense of an organized drill. He then quietly told the crew, minus Curly, about the prank that *they* were gonna pull on that long haired cowboy. It was explained that Curly was in the kitchen playing the part of the victim in what he thinks is a Company first aid drill. The crew was gonna go in just like they would at an emergency, check out this unconscious victim and start giving him basic first aid for his injuries. But instead, on a signal from the Captain, the plan was for all of them to pin Curly down while the Captain cut off some of his hair. Everybody agreed it was a great plan. In the interest of keeping the rookie out of it, he was told he could watch but not to get directly involved.

When the crew went into the kitchen they found Fireman Curly laying face up on the kitchen table dutifully playing his part as the injured victim. The crew quickly surrounded him, and when given the signal, they quit pretending about first aid and securely pinned his arms and legs down to the table. Curly then played his part to the hilt by putting up a hell of a struggle while the Captain got out a noisy pair of electric shears and started cutting locks of his hair off. Finally the Captain told the guys to let him go, and up jumped their furious victim. After ranting and raving against his tormentors, Curly stormed out of the kitchen's only door and disappeared. While laughing at the results of their successful prank, the crew assumed that their victim had probably gone back to the bathroom mirror to check out the damage that had been done. But, in a moment, Curly burst back through the kitchen's screened doors with a crazy look on his face and a large caliber revolver in his hand.

Before this double cross gotten started, both Fireman Mel and Curly had made some important pre-prank preparations. Mel had fashioned a tin foil pouch full of catsup that he had attached to his chest, underneath his white T-shirt. And, *the gun nut* had made up some blanks for his pistol with wads of tissue paper replacing the slugs.

Everybody in 45's kitchen froze as Curly stood just inside the doorway waving his gun around and challenging the crew's manhood. Then, Mel broke the crew's shocked silence with a snide, "Kiss my ass Curly, you ain't gonna shoot anybody". **BANG!** The room reverberated with the noise from the gun as he promptly shot Mel. Seated across the room, Fireman Mel reacted very convincingly. The wadding from the blank had slammed into his arm so hard that he actually thought for a moment that he had been shot. But, he still had the presence of mind to slap his chest with his hand. Bright red catsup immediately darkened his shirt and squirted out between his fingers. At that point, pandemonium broke loose among the four members of the crew that were not in on this part of the prank.

With Curly standing just inside the only doorway, gun still in hand, these four guys were trapped in the dead end of the kitchen. And, each one of them took their own defensive actions.

The rookie was able to wedge most of himself in behind the refrigerator. This was a large commercial-like unit and way too heavy for one guy to move and only had a sliver of room behind it. But, the rookie almost completely squeezed himself behind it. The Engineer kinda went into shock and pressed himself back down into a small space between the stove and the sink. All the time mumbling the same thing over and over, "Mel's dead, Mel's dead". Another fireman went for the only window in that end of the kitchen. It was right above where the mumbling Engineer was *hiding* and was way too small for him to get out of. But, that didn't stop him, as he stepped all over the Engineer's head and shoulders while trying to get through it.

The last guy, who was just back from the Korean War, was the only one to consider some kinda offensive action against the shooter. With his adrenaline pumpin', he turned over the big heavy wooden kitchen table, picking it up from underneath and holding it out in front of himself like a shield. He remembers thinking to himself at that moment, *'that after surviving some of the most murderous combat of the War without a scratch, he was now gonna be shot down at the fire station'*. He was also considering charging the shooter with his table if Curly had of pointed the gun in his direction.

Meanwhile, the Captain was still workin' the prank for all it was worth. "Calm down now Curly, just give me the gun". And, Fireman Mel was still bleeding catsup badly and moaning loudly, while observing all the action.

At that point, Curly slowly handed the Captain his gun, and two of the guys in the dead end of the kitchen made a break for the door. As they went running by, Curly just couldn't resist grabbing the gun back from the Captain and firing off a couple of more blanks at his fleeing fire buds through the swinging screen doors. At this point the prank ended. While Curly and Mel collapsed in laughter, the Captain took off after his two panicked crew members to stop'em before they got out of the engine house. He did manage to catch'em, but just barely. Asked later where they were going. One said that he was "gonna keep on runnin' until he found a cop".

After everybody finally calmed down, they all had a grand ol' time rehashin' all the fun and excitement they'd just experienced. But then, the Engineer started having pains in his chest. This concerned everybody, so the Captain had him taken over to a local hospital and quietly checked out. Thankfully the Engineer checked out all right, and returned to finish out the shift. But his pains reappeared at home the next day, and he got scared and called the Battalion Chief. This chief was stationed nearby and came right over, picked him up, and ran him down to L.A. City's old Central Receiving Hospital. In route the Engineer spilled the beans on the actual cause of his problem. At the hospital he was taken into an examination room and checked over by a City doctor. And after a bit, he also had to tell the Doctor his story. The Doctor, in turn, left him to go out and talk to the Battalion Chief waiting in the hall. "Have you heard this man's story, Chief?" When the Chief said he had, the astonished doctor pressed him further, "and you believe him?"

It turned out that the Engineer was only suffering from some kind of a anxiety attack which could have been cured by most any tranquilizer. But the cat was now out of the bag, as the story even appeared in the L.A. Times about these Firemen titled, *"The Shoot out at 45's"*.

In a week or so the Department convened a 'Board of Rights' to find out what really happened and properly punish any wrongdoers. Fire Station 45 was closed for the day as the entire crew was transported down to Headquarters. A panel of 3 chief officers then called in each member one at a time to hear his story, starting with the rookie. They interviewed the three perpetrators last, and all three of the Chiefs had some serious trouble keeping their laughter under control while hearing each one of their stories. The result of this inquiry was Curly and Fireman Mel both got 3 shifts off without pay, and the Captain got about twice that. Also, both Curly and the Captain were transferred to other fire stations in the City. These penalties that were agreeable to all, considering all the brass that got involved.

- YOUR FAVORITE PRANK -

I'm sure, after reading this book, a lot of you firemen out there will think of a couple of good fire house pranks that you feel should've been included in this book. And I agree with ya!

There are millions of firemen and thousands of fire stations across this diverse country of ours, so no way did I think I could cover every aspect of fire house pranks from just my experience in the fire service. I mean, I've never worked at a station in a harbor, or at an airport, or even in the snow. So, obviously, there is a deep well of great stories out there about activities I haven't even touched upon. This is where you come in. If you looked at the title closely, you noticed that this edition of the *Lil' Red Book of Fire House Pranks* is Vol. I. Hopefully, additional volumes will be published in the future as more material is collected. I'm hopping that my best source of these fire house prank stories will come from you. So, please contact me if you've got a good one!

Please tear out the last page in this book, fill it out, and mail it to me.....Then, I'll contact you for the details of your story. If your fire house tale is included in one of the up coming volumes, both you and your fire department will be given credit. Plus, I'll gladly send ya a free book, and 50% off any additional books you may want. The rich history and tradition of *rollin' a fire house turd* is quickly becoming a thing of the past. So, it's important to get that aspect of fire house life on record while memories are still fresh from *the good old days.*

Thanks for your help!
Jeff Hibbard

MAIL TO: FIRE HOUSE PRANKS
13237 Sierra Highway
Saugus, CA 91350

name_____

address_____

_____

phone: Daytime_____

               Evenings_____

Best time to call_____Retired or Active?_____

Name of your Fire Dept._____

Please give brief description of prank:

-use other side or other sheets if needed-